# Take Courage!

## Growing Stronger
## after
## Losing Your Spouse

with contributions from:

Bruce McLeod
Rev. Gary Vossler, M.Div
Joy Ost
Linda Smith, BS
Lisa Greene, MA, CFLE
Mary Beth Woll, MA, LMHC
Nancy Honeytree Miller
Chaplain Roberta Reyna, MA
Ruth Martinez (Ost)

# ENDORSEMENTS

I can't think of a better title for a book than *Take Courage!*. The first words I heard from God after my husband of almost 28 years and ministry partner, best friend, and confidant passed away was, "Courage brings clarity, cowardliness brings confusion." I was to walk in courage, in order to have the direction I was going to need for the days ahead. The power that comes from the encouragement and practical how-to suggestions from people that have walked where you are walking is tangible and life-giving for us that are left to start anew. To hear the struggles and successes gives reality and confidence that we can make it as well. For it to be reinforced that crying is not just ok but encouraged is healing in itself; and to be released to apply what you can from the book in the speed and timing that is good for you, is the best advice ever. Linda, Mary Beth, Nancy, Bruce, Ruth, and the other authors were blessings from God just when I needed it the most. Thank you all from the bottom of my heart for your transparency, faithfulness, and love.

*Pattie Klewer*
*Pastor's Wife, Singles Co-Pastor for 27 years*
*New Covenant Church, Longview, Texas*

I have many friends here in Mexico who are mourning for loved ones who have passed away. They are trying to find words of comfort to soothe their deep pain. *Take Courage!* will satisfy their need. It helps the reader realize that it is beneficial to grieve, to cry, to ask for help, and to take care of ourselves. The authors are very articulate in explaining not only how to process normal grief, but they also explain how to process complicated grief. They share what they have learned by living through their own experiences of grief. I highly recommend *Take Courage!* for all those who want to find empathy and courage. Thank you very much for encouraging me in my grief journey.

*Ruth Avendaño, Administrator in*
*ACCOMPANYING LEGACY - COMFORTED TO COMFORT*

It is with great appreciation and anticipation that I endorse *Take Courage!* written in part by two sisters in widowhood. Having studied Don't Lose Heart!, this great addition to their writing will encourage all widows and widowers as they journey through the difficult steps of being widowed.

These authors know first hand what the journey is all about. The various topics of *Take Courage!* will speak to the many challenges each of the widowed will face. Through God's Word they verify what God's teachings are about living widowed. The pain is real, and this book will address your sorrow and what is needed to live after being widowed.

*Cindy Rose*
*Seattle Widows President*

This book flows from the experience of real people, who suffered real loss, who found real encouragement, in real time, from a real and present God. As I read the reflections, testimonies, and advice from these authors, I recognized the fulfilled promise of 2 Corinthians 1:3-5:

> Praise be to the God and Father of our Lord Jesus Christ, the Father of compassion and the God of all comfort, who comforts us in all our troubles, so that we can comfort those in any trouble with the comfort we ourselves receive from God. For just as we share abundantly in the sufferings of Christ, so also our comfort abounds through Christ.

The authors of this volume suffered great loss, experienced comfort from God, and now find the Holy Spirit's strength to help others through their personal experiences. I commend this volume to you, as well as the ministry of The Widows Project. You will find inspiration and instruction.

*Rev. Leslie E. Welk*
*Ministry Resources International Pastoral Counselor*
*Former Northwest Ministry Network Superintendent*

Thank you for walking through that valley of the shadow with me—and others—holding our hearts and steadying our feeble knees with listening ears and helping hands. You have helped me see grief as both affliction and antidote, finding hope and rest for our souls.

*Charlene Baldwin*
*Author, Bible Teacher, Missionary, Pastor's Wife*

Mary Beth Woll and Linda Smith have spearheaded the publishing of a great book on grief and widowhood. Nine authors share their personal experiences on becoming widowed. They give great personal insights into their own journeys. The chapters are filled with personal struggles and victories in navigating their lives. They ask great questions at the end of each chapter for reflection by the reader on their own life.

I have known Mary Beth for many years as her pastor and friend. I have watched her live what she teaches. She and Linda Smith help lead The Widows Project and have a great heart for the widowed. Mary Beth and Linda are godly women full of Christ's character. Read it and weep (in a healing way) and be helped and strengthened. I highly recommend this book.

*Dr. Dan C. Hammer*
*Sonrise Christian Center*
*Senior Apostolic Leader*
*President, Seattle Bible College*

# TAKE
## *Courage!*

GROWING STRONGER
AFTER LOSING YOUR SPOUSE

A COLLABORATIVE BOOK BY NINE INTERNATIONAL AUTHORS.

EDITED BY LINDA SMITH, BS AND MARY BETH WOLL, MA, LMHC

All scriptures quoted are taken from the
New International Version of the Bible
unless otherwise indicated.

ISBN: 978-0-578-81981-5
Cover Design: David Woll
Interior Layout/Self-Publishing: Kristi Knowles

# DEDICATION

To the widowed of the world,
we love you!
With God's help,
you're going to make it!

Love,

The *Take Courage!* authors,
and The Widows Project

# ACKNOWLEDGEMENTS

### Rolland Wright
Thank you for your visionary leadership in founding
The Widows Project. You have changed so many lives around
the world and have cut a path for others to follow. Thank you!

### Ruth Ost Martinez
Thank you for dreaming about each author writing one chapter,
"and then we'll put them all together in a book."
You are so often divinely inspired!

### Nancy Honeytree Miller
Thank you so much for the concept of this collaborative
book and for bringing all the authors together.
What a God thing!

### The authors of *Take Courage!*
Thank you for your heartfelt contributions born out
of your own grief and loss, and for persevering
through pain to bring comfort to countless others.

### Kristi Knowles, our amazing publisher
You are awesome! Your gifts and talents, offered to
God and to us, have made this work possible.
Thank you so much!

### David Woll, graphic artist
Your excellent creativity and expertise in designing
the cover and interior graphics of this book have
given us an inspiring and comforting visual.
Thank you so much for lending your talents
to the widowed of the world.

# FOREWORD

by Rev. Mark Ost, Missionary to France

I am so glad to present to you this book, **Take Courage! Growing Stronger after Losing Your Spouse**. I have been a pastor and shepherd over different flocks in various cultural settings for 44 years. I have always been intrigued by learning to comfort and accompany church members and their extended families through deep grief as they have laid their loved ones to rest.

I have been present with more than a hundred people as they have taken their last breath. Then I have had the responsibility to help their loved ones through the "Valley of the Shadow of Death." I tend to them until they are at peace and ready to comfort others in the same distress.

Then I received a call from my sister, Ruth Martinez, a missionary in Mexico who lost her husband Victor the year before. She told me she was reaching out to comfort other widows who had lost their husbands during the Covid pandemic, even as the Lord was comforting her own broken heart through the ministry of The Widows Project. She was preparing to train teams to reach out to hundreds of women. However, she kept hearing of dozens of men who had lost their wives and also needed care.

She asked me to help her figure out how to get men to reach out to widowers. I immediately told her that I would contact a few pastors. I was sure that we would soon have a group of men who would be willing to minister to widowers.

Great was my surprise, however, as I heard the replies of these pastors. Although they were in ministry, because they had not been widowed, they felt inadequate to walk alongside those who were grieving. And who could blame them? No denomination or church family in the world had anticipated or was prepared for a pandemic that would cause thousands of families to know sudden grief!

These pastors found it difficult to comfort men who were crying after losing their wives. How could they help them come to a place of peace until they could eventually say, "Okay Pastor, I truly feel that it is well with my soul. Now, who can I comfort?"

For six months, nine international authors, including Ruth and me, met online with Mary Beth Woll and Linda Smith to study their book ***Don't Lose Heart!***. These women taught us what they had learned as they lived out their own widowhood. * We soon realized that ministering to grieving men and women would be a long-term commitment. Using social networks, we established a virtual weekly meeting for widows and widowers.

From this group sprang the idea that we needed to collaborate to write a book which would specifically address the first critical year after losing a spouse. We needed to provide emotional "first aid" to those in grief, operating as "first responders" in their lives. Authors in Mexico and the United States put their hands to the task, showing the Father's compassion as they shared from personal experiences. They each wrote about themes that are vital to the first days and weeks after losing a loved one. Week by week, one of our nine authors presented a new chapter of *Take Courage!* to the group. Then we broke into small groups, shared together, cried together, and prayed for one another.

The book you hold in your hands was written as we taught, comforted, and welcomed new individuals suffering from grief. It was so exciting to realize how the Lord had miraculously comforted and equipped those of us who shared a sole desire: that of comforting others with the comfort that we ourselves had received from God (2 Corinthians 1:3-5).

Many of the people in the team that God brought together were comforting others even as they, themselves, were being comforted from day to day. We learned so much together. We saw God's anointing on our lives, bringing about the healing of broken hearts. We truly lived out the purpose of the Church as stated in Isaiah 61:1-3:

> The Spirit of the Sovereign LORD is on me, because the LORD has anointed me to proclaim good news to the poor. He has sent me to bind up the brokenhearted, to proclaim freedom for the captives and release from darkness for the prisoners, to proclaim the year of the LORD's favor and the day of vengeance of our God, to comfort all who mourn, and provide

for those who grieve in Zion— to bestow on them a crown of beauty instead of ashes, the oil of joy instead of mourning, and a garment of praise instead of a spirit of despair. They will be called oaks of righteousness, a planting of the LORD for the display of his splendor.

Living out this Scripture became our goal as we prayed, we loved, and we gave of our time. We followed up on group members by listening with sensitive hearts to long phone conversations, valuing each individual story. We set up smaller groups to edify and comfort each other. We watched the Lord draw men and women to Himself. We knew that ultimately He is the only One who could bring comfort that lasts.

To facilitate this effort, my sister, Ruth, recruited people to help her translate each chapter of **Take Courage!** to Spanish. At times, Mary Beth and Linda taught through translators. Authors and pastors Bruce, Gary, Ellis, and I adapted the chapters for the men we were reaching each week. A couple of the widowed pastors in the groups participated by giving their testimonies about how the Lord had "turned their mourning into dancing" (Psalm 30:11, KJV).

As of this writing, we have been able to minister directly to over 850 widows and 100 widowers. I pray that this book will make us aware that as we have received comfort from God, He has also given us the capacity to comfort others. This world is full of people who need us to comfort and encourage them. May we all be found as faithful workers in God's Harvest, as we commit to comforting others with His Word and the wonderful promise that He will be with us always, "to the very end of the age" (Matthew 28:20).

*Rev. Mark Ost*
*Missionary to France, Pastor of Faith, Hope, and Love Church*
*Greater Paris Metropolitan Region*

* I have also commissioned **Don't Lose Heart!** to be translated into the French language. Our intent is to soon open "Comforted to Comfort Others" online groups in France and across the French-speaking world.

# Table of Contents

# Take Courage!

Growing Stronger
after
Losing Your Spouse

# Chapter 1

*Is it Okay to Cry?*
*By Ruth Martinez*

It was 6:00 p.m. on Sunday. I opened my bedroom door, once again, to face the heartbreaking reality that Victor, my partner of 48 years, would never come back. His side of the bed would be empty forever. He would no longer sit in his favorite living room chair. Our dreams of growing old together would never come true.

Victor and I had planned to leave on a three-month ministry trip, but then he died. I was left with so many questions. "Why me? Why now? What will become of me? When will this sharp, intense pain ever end?"

My mind went back 34 and 36 years to when I experienced the loss of my father and mother in a two-year period. The pain was deep, but my husband comforted me. My five children and the ministry demanded my attention. At that time, crying was frowned upon. We were told that we must be strong.

I was now immersed in the deepest pain of my life. My beloved husband, my protector, my provider, the man who made me laugh every day, who hugged and encouraged me, my best friend was gone. He knew me so well. I was always free to cry with him. I was overwhelmed with the flood of tears that came over me. I felt the intense pain caused by the departure of the person with whom I had been one for so many years.

I asked myself, "Who am I now? What's next?"

As the weeks passed, the reality of my new life as a widow hit me with increasing intensity. No one understood me except my sister Joy, who had lost her husband many years prior. Joy called me every day. No one else welcomed me to the Widows' Club. What heartbreaking and inexplicable pain! How could I get through this valley of tears? How long would this agony last?

I was a vulnerable woman, alone and unprotected. I felt lonely. I felt unsafe. We were no longer a couple. Our married friends quietly stayed away. The future now seemed so bleak.

What was I going to do? I asked myself, "Who am I? Why am I here? What can I do? Is there still a purpose for my life?" I felt like my heart broke into thousands of pieces. Tears of remorse inundated my soul! I was flooded with thoughts of guilt and resentment: "If only I hadn't said... If only I had done...."

Amid my suffering, I wondered, "How much longer can I endure this pain and these tears? If I have God the Father, God the Son, and God the Holy Spirit living in me, is it really okay to cry?"

As Son of God and Son of Man, Jesus is the only one who can understand us in every difficult moment of our lives. In John 11, we find that even Jesus wept when His friend, Lazarus, died. He was deeply moved. Although Jesus knew that He would raise Lazarus from the dead, He first took time to weep with Lazarus' friends and family, Mary, and Martha.

We will cry while here on earth. We will walk through the valley of tears. Only in eternity will we experience the glorious moment when God Himself wipes every tear from our eyes.

There is a time to cry! It is of great comfort and strength in times of pain to read God's Word that says, "You keep track of all my sorrows. You have collected all my tears in Your bottle. You have recorded each one in Your book" (Psalm 56:8).

Psalm 139 speaks of a God so personal that my mind cannot conceive of Him. He has numbered the hairs on my head. He hears my deepest sighs. God has been keenly aware of every detail of my life since I was conceived in my mother's womb.

The book of Psalms contains more than 50 references to weeping, wailing, sobbing, and crying out to God. In the Old Testament, people wept and took time to grieve and mourn.

The Bible says that Jesus Himself, who understands all our weaknesses, was tempted in everything, but without sin. Society tells us that crying is a sign of weakness, especially among men: "Big boys don't cry." But, as Hebrews 5:7 says, when Jesus walked the earth, "He had offered up prayers and supplications with strong crying and tears unto Him that was able to save Him from death."

You may ask how I have managed my grief since Victor died.

I have cried deeply and intensely! I have cried in front of my children and grandchildren. All they could do was to hug me and cry with me. My soul found rest when I intentionally wept out loud. I discovered God to be "the God of all comfort who comforts us in all our affliction" (2 Corinthians 1:4 ESV).

> M̲y soul found rest when I intentionally wept out loud.

On my six-month anniversary as a widow, between tears and sobs, I was able to raise my arms to God and say, "Thank You for taking my husband. Thank You for leaving me here as a widow." This expression freed my soul from its anguish and grief. I was able to say, "Your plans and purposes are perfect, even though I will not understand them on this side of eternity."

In the Beatitudes, Jesus taught, "Blessed are those who mourn, for they shall be comforted" (Matthew 5:4). Though we may not know what to do or say, the Apostle Paul commands us to mourn with those who mourn (Romans 12:15).

To my surprise, I discovered that when I seemed to be coming down with the flu or a headache, or when I felt like I'd been hit by a train, I just needed a good cry. At times like this, I played sad songs like, "Will you Hold me While I Cry?" This brought me to tears and I cried from the depths of my soul. Sobs welled up from my innermost being, and I cried until I couldn't cry anymore.

In this passing world, we will probably never know the "why" behind tragedies, deaths, diseases, betrayals, disasters, and things that cause deep heartache and pain. But there is a "what for." 2 Corinthians 1:3-5 says:

> Blessed be the God and Father of our Lord Jesus Christ, the Father of mercies and God of all comfort, who comforts us in all our affliction so that we will be able to comfort those who are in any trouble with the comfort we ourselves have received from God. For just as the sufferings of Christ are ours in abundance, so also our comfort is abundant through Christ.

Psalm 30:5 says that "weeping may endure for a night, but joy comes in the morning."

The Amplified Bible says God:

> "comforts and encourages us in every trouble so that we will be able to comfort and encourage those who are in any kind of trouble with the comfort with which we ourselves are comforted by God" (2 Corinthians 1:4).

Through my tears, I can now repeat, "We know that all things work together for good for those who love God, who are called according to His purpose" (Romans 8:28).

Looking back, when my parents passed away, I came to know God in another dimension as a tender, loving, rich, and perfect Father who loves me deeply as His daughter. Now that my husband is gone, I have come to know God as my Husband. He is by my side as my Advisor, my Guide, my Intercessor, my Helper, and my Resource, should I need anything else!

Only God knew how many people I would soon encounter who had lost their spouses after I did. They would also need comfort during their pain. I have decided to embrace my new purpose as a widow and comfort others with the comfort I have received from God.

I had a purpose when I was single. I had a purpose as a wife for 48 years. I have a purpose as a mother, a grandmother, and a great-grandmother. Now, I have a purpose as a widow. The words of Isaiah 61:1 burn in my soul, "The Spirit of the Lord is upon me because he has sent me to heal the brokenhearted." My prayer is that my experience will help you know that you, too, can find the comfort that comes from God and His purpose for you at this stage of your life.

# Questions for Discussion:

1.  What do you do when you are confronted with thoughts of guilt about crying? Why do you feel guilty about crying?

    _____

    _____

    _____

    _____

    _____

    _____

    _____

    _____

    _____

2.  Have you taken time to cry? Consider Psalm 56:8 (NASB), "You have taken account of my miseries; put my tears in Your bottle. Are they not in Your book?"

    _____

    _____

    _____

    _____

    _____

    _____

    _____

    _____

    _____

3. Have you allowed other people you trust to cry with you? Have you allowed them to hug you?

_____

_____

_____

_____

_____

_____

_____

_____

_____

_____

4. How do you feel about giving thanks to God for allowing you to be widowed?

_____

_____

_____

_____

_____

_____

_____

_____

_____

_____

5. My new purpose, as a widow, is to pass along the comfort God has given me and to bind up the broken hearted (2 Corinthians 1:4, Isaiah 61:1). Do you see a new purpose emerging from your grief?

_____

_____

_____

_____

_____

_____

_____

6. Rewrite Psalm 139 in the first person, substituting your own name in the verses, to remind yourself of God's personal care for you.

_____

_____

_____

_____

_____

_____

_____

_____

_____

I want to encourage you to cry until you find rest in your soul. Cry long, hard, and deep. The Bible encourages us that, "Weeping endures for the night, but joy comes in the morning" (Psalm 30:5).

# Chapter 2
## *I Forgive*
### *by Joy Ost*

My husband Isaí and I had only been married 21 months when I received the tragic news that he had been killed in a car accident. Isaí was a founding member of a contemporary Christian rock band created in the mid-seventies. The band was traveling from Monterrey, Mexico, to play at a friend's wedding in Brownsville, Texas. A driver ran two stop signs and crashed into the back of their van. Isaí was killed instantly, and his brother-in-law died two days later. One group member walked away with barely a scratch, and another spent several days in the hospital.

I was left alone to raise our 11-month-old daughter, Damaris. Our beautiful child, the joy and pride of Isaí's life, was now fatherless. My sister-in-law was left to raise their 6-month-old son.

Because Isaí's band was well-known across Mexico and beyond, we had a huge funeral. I cried so many tears that I thought it would be impossible to cry any more, but they just kept coming.

Five months into my experience of widowhood, I received a phone call from my father. He said that my mother was about to undergo an 11-hour brain surgery. The doctors had warned my parents that Mom's surgery might not go well; there was a possibility that she could be left deaf or dumb because of the surgery. In the worst-case scenario, Mom might not survive. I immediately flew to Minneapolis to be with them. By God's grace, my mother came through the surgery with excellent results.

A few years later, my father was called to heaven. My mother followed him in less than two years. Within an eight-year period, my husband, my father, and my mother were gone. I had never felt so all alone in my entire life.

Subconsciously, I was mad at God, and I thought God was mad at me. I wondered if God was punishing me; maybe I did not deserve to be happily married and enjoy our little daughter.

Had God singled me out to suffer more than anyone else in my family?

Before this tragedy happened, I had glibly repeated Romans 8:28, which says, "And we know that in all things, God works for the good of those who love Him, who have been called according to His purpose." I thought God would be forced to reward and bless me, but amid these hard times, I did not see God's goodness.

One day, a friend wisely advised me that I was mad at God. This revelation hit me like a ton of bricks! I was also confronted with my need to forgive God, other people, and even myself. I woke up to the fact that God was not mad at me. In fact, God loved me.

Isaí's death was not God's punishment. Although we all suffer grief and hardship, because I belonged to God, I knew He would turn around even this tragedy for my good.

I began to understand that although forgiveness is a major theme in the Bible, I had not yet learned to forgive. So, I decided to focus on it. I came to understand that forgiveness is a choice. It is not a magic pill I can swallow and wake up to discover that my anger is gone. Forgiveness is an act of my will. By forgiving, I take responsibility for my own reactions.

After enduring the losses of my husband and parents, I thought I was entitled to a life free from further suffering. However, I experienced another test when, at age 21, my daughter was diagnosed with cancer. Damaris almost lost her right leg and went through 12 major surgeries in 10 years. Would I blame God for this cancer or choose to trust Him? As I resolved to trust God and, once again, embrace Romans 8:28, I could see that He was working everything together for good. Damaris has now been cancer-free for over 21 years.

When I suffered, I thought God was treating me unjustly and bringing tragedies upon me. However, Jesus told His disciples, "In this world you will have trouble" (John 16:33). That's just the nature of life on Planet Earth. I have learned that life is not fair, but God will always walk with me through calamity. Jesus goes on to say, "But take heart! I have overcome the world." He is always by my side, even in times of trouble. I may not see Him, but He is there.

Over time I have learned the power of declaring my faith in God by such statements as:

- Nothing can separate me from God's love.
- I choose to give up regret and despair.
- I choose to forgive because God commands me to.

I have learned to make a list of grievances including the names of the people who have hurt me. I think about the offenses and let them go—one by one—saying, "I forgive." No one else can forgive for me, so I choose to forgive.

Forgiving is not easy. I have learned that being a follower of Christ requires me to take action. At one point, I had so much anger in my heart towards someone that the only way I could let it go was to humble myself. I got down on my knees and washed their feet.

> *I came to understand that forgiveness is a choice. It is not a magic pill I can swallow and wake up to discover that my anger is gone. Forgiveness is an act of my will. By forgiving, I take responsibility for my own reactions.*

Another action is to develop a lifestyle of reading the Bible and praying daily. These spiritual disciplines require a strong commitment. By developing them, I become spiritually prepared for whatever adversity may come my way.

Forgiveness is also good for me. Hanging on to anger, nursing grudges, and justifying my reactions does nothing but damage my soul. So, I decided to forgive everyone for everything. I repeated the words "I forgive" so often that when I dug into my heart to bring up old hurts and grudges, they weren't there anymore.

Experience has taught me that if I choose to harbor anger in my heart, it affects me the most. People who have hurt me usually just go on living, while I am left behind seething. It is up to me to decide to:

1. face the anger,
2. acknowledge the hurt,
3. forgive the offender, and then

4. let it go.

I am the person who benefits the most from this forgiveness process.

How could I not forgive everyone, when all my suffering could never compare to the agony and pain that Jesus endured for me? He was maligned, misunderstood, betrayed by His best friends, humiliated, dehumanized, degraded, and beaten. He was stripped of His dignity in the cruelest way imaginable with the endorsement of the religious leaders. Ultimately, Jesus hung on the cross and died to pay for the forgiveness of my sins.

Forgiveness is also good for my health. Studies at Johns Hopkins Hospital have found that:

> ...the act of forgiveness can reap huge rewards for my health, lowering the risk of heart attack; improving cholesterol levels and sleep; and reducing pain, blood pressure, and levels of anxiety, depression, and stress... unresolved conflict can go deeper than you may realize— it may be affecting your physical health. Forgiveness, however, calms stress levels, leading to improved health.[1]

I also learned that I must forgive myself. It is easier for me to forgive others while I hold a grudge against myself for my failures. I sometimes list my failures and the things I find so hard to forgive. The only way to remedy my past and move on with compassion for myself is to:

1. accept responsibility for what I did,
2. apologize to the person I offended (if possible),
3. focus on what I learned from the experience, and
4. continuously choose to forgive myself.

Because forgiving is often difficult, I find myself repeating, "I forgive, I forgive, I forgive." It seems to drain the anger and resentment from my soul. I remind myself again and again that the decision is mine. I am the person who benefits the most from my choice to forgive, knowing that my forgiveness is an act of my will. So, I decide to forgive because Jesus commanded it, and it also benefits me.

---

1     "Forgiveness: Your Health Depends on It." *Johns Hopkins Medicine*, www.hopkinsmedicine.org/health/wellness-and-prevention/forgiveness-your-health-depends-on-it.

# Questions for Discussion:

1. Who is the first person you forgave after the death of your spouse?

_____

_____

_____

_____

_____

_____

_____

_____

2. Can you think of anyone you need to forgive?

_____

_____

_____

_____

_____

_____

_____

_____

_____

_____

3. Can you think of anything for which you need to forgive yourself?

_____

_____

_____

_____

_____

_____

_____

_____

_____

_____

# Chapter 3
*Fear Not!*
*by Mary Beth Woll, MA, LMHC*

The Bible contains many encouragements to "Fear Not!" When announcing Jesus' birth, the angel said to Mary, "Fear not! I bring you good tidings of great joy that shall be for all people" (Luke 2:10). Jesus said to His disciples, "Do not let your hearts be troubled. Trust in God. Trust also in me" (John 14:1). Jesus also comforts us in John 14:27: "Peace I leave with you; My peace I give you. I do not give to you as the world gives. Do not let your hearts be troubled and do not be afraid." He continues in John 16:33, "In this world you will have trouble. But take heart! I have overcome the world."

In Psalm 23, King David reminds us that the Good Shepherd is with us as we walk through the Valley of the Shadow of Death. We need not fear evil for He is with us! I Peter 5:7 says to "Cast all your cares upon Him, for He cares for you!" Isaiah 41:10 says, "Fear not, for I am with you; do not be dismayed, for I am your God. I will strengthen you and help you. I will uphold you with My righteous right hand." Joshua 1:9 says, "Be strong and courageous. Do not be terrified, do not be discouraged, for the Lord your God will be with you wherever you go."

So, if God is with us and the Holy Spirit is in us, why would we suffer anxiety and fear at the death of a spouse?

> *Isaiah 41:10 says, "Fear not, for I am with you; do not be dismayed, for I am your God. I will strengthen you and help you. I will uphold you with My righteous right hand."*

I have first-hand experience with such anxiety. When I lost my husband Bob, I was so overwhelmed that all I could feel was devastation, shock, and numbness. My condition was like that of a person sitting by the side of a road following a car accident. The paramedics arrive, wrap a blanket around the dazed victim, and remove them from the scene so they can begin to recover. They may not remember a thing that happened during the crash. This shock is God's anesthetic from the initial, crushing pain. But, at some point, the numbness fades and the feelings emerge.

Immediately after Bob died, I was just so grateful that he was with Jesus. God helped us navigate the crisis of Bob's critical illness and passing. Bob and I had crossed the finish line of "'til death do us part" with fierce love and faithfulness. Although he was gone, I was positive that Bob didn't want to leave me. He fought with every ounce of his strength and faith to stay. And our entire family and friends fought with him. In the end, it was God's timing for Bob to go to be with Jesus. Though shocked and confused, we accepted that our almighty and infinitely good Heavenly Father had a purpose for taking Bob to Heaven. Bob's physical and emotional suffering was over. He was instantly experiencing more peace and happiness in Heaven with Jesus than he ever, ever could have shared with me on this earth. Though devastated by the loss of my lifetime love, I was so grateful for God's miraculous presence throughout Bob's "Valley of the Shadow of Death" (Psalm 23:4).

And then, we all went home.

My family came with me, but Bob wasn't there. Though we could all envision him walking in the front door, reality began to sink in. Bob would never come home again.

Family and friends stayed with me, but after a while, they returned to their own lives. I soon discovered that I couldn't tolerate being home alone. Because I had gone straight from my parents' home to college and then marriage, I suddenly realized that I had never lived alone in my life. I was inexplicably terrified in the house where Bob and I had lived and loved for 26 ½ years. There we had raised our four children and welcomed eight grandchildren. I was certain that if I allowed myself to experience these unprecedented, agonizing emotions, I would surely die! I was facing the deepest grief of my life without my greatest comforter, Bob, to hold me as I sobbed gut-wrenching tears. I expected to feel unspeakably sad. I was completely surprised by anxiety! For six months, I traveled between the homes of my children, my sister, and close friends.

Further, I didn't know that I was seriously ill with severe anemia when Bob died. I had so focused on caregiving that I had neglected to take care of myself. I was so extremely weak that I couldn't climb a short flight of stairs or cook for myself. I thought this overwhelming fatigue was "just grief." After a couple of weeks, my son finally took me to a doctor who, upon testing, immediately sent me to the hospital for blood transfusions. Our entire family had experienced such trauma during Bob's hospitalization that I begged the doctor not to admit me. How could my children bear to see their only remaining parent in the hospital? After one transfusion, the doctor reluctantly released me. Within a few days, however, I was admitted for more transfusions and testing.

After being released from the hospital and multiple trips to the emergency room, my friend and fellow widow, Linda Smith, invited me to stay with her for one week. After a week, we realized that I was still not yet strong enough to live alone. Though I was slowly gaining strength, I recognized that depression and anxiety had compounded my grief. Linda encouraged me to stay with her until I was well. She also fed me a well-balanced diet.

I made an appointment with a psychiatrist and began a course of medication for anxiety and depression. I pursued my healing by meeting with a therapist, a grief counselor, a financial planner, and a massage therapist. I also began exercising regularly as my strength allowed.

But I was not aware that a spiritual force was also involved. I now know that the enemy of our souls was also at work. True to his mission to steal, kill and destroy, the devil did not relent in his efforts just because I was a grieving widow. That's when I realized that he is such an opportunistic criminal that he will kick ANYBODY when they are down—the more vulnerable, the better!

I attempted unsuccessfully to go home. I trembled at my own doorstep! I called my sister, Joanna, to pray with me before I could step over the threshold. Overcome with grief and fear, I could only tolerate being home for an hour or two before I would have to leave. Little by little, I increased the time spent there until I could stay the night. But because I was completely exhausted after every attempt, I continued to stay with Linda for 3 ½ months as I gained strength.

Finally, about six months after Bob's passing, I visited my sister, Joanna, and her husband James who were pastoring a church about two hours from my home. I cried out to God as I drove, "Dear God, I need a breakthrough! I need a word from You!" I so badly wanted to go home but felt paralyzed by fear and exhaustion.

Because it was early December, James was preaching a Christmas sermon. The title of his sermon was "Fear Not!" James told the story from Luke 1:30 about the angel Gabriel visiting Mary to announce the birth of Jesus.

James asked the congregation, "What did Gabriel say to Mary?" Then, he responded to his own question, pointed directly at me, and loudly declared "Fear not, Mary!"

A second time, James pointed directly at me and said, "Fear not, Mary!"

I knew I had received my word from God! I was so hoping that James would open the altar after the service because I couldn't wait to go up for prayer! James did open the altar! He led the way, followed closely by Joanna, then me! James so sweetly and gently counseled me. Then, as he prayed, the spirit of fear that had so bound me was instantly gone! Jesus set me free!

Later, James told me that he didn't realize he had pointed directly at me! But God was orchestrating the events of the evening in answer to my cry for help!

When I returned to Linda's house, she was amazed at the difference in me. "Before you left, all you could say was, 'Bob's not here. Bob's not here.' Now, all you can say is, 'God is with me!'"

I stayed one more week with Linda, then on December 13—exactly six months after Bob died—I went home with absolutely NO FEAR! And that spirit of fear has not returned!

Each person's grief journey is unique. I know that many widows have suffered unspeakably more than I have. Yet, I was overcome with physical, psychological, emotional, social, and spiritual challenges which required the help of my family, friends, and church. It also required medical and divine intervention. Is it any wonder that James 1:27 says that "Religion that God our

Father accepts as pure and faultless is to look after orphans and widows in their distress"? I was so helpless that I would not have survived alone. But God provided the help I needed! Now, my experience of utter devastation has given me great empathy for other widows who are similarly suffering. I really do understand them. As 2 Corinthians 1:4 says, because I was comforted in my affliction, I can now comfort others with the comfort I have received from God. I can relate to widows who are experiencing overwhelming anxiety and fear. I can empathize and encourage them to "Fear not!" as they recover from their losses.

# Questions for Discussion:

Please remember that anxiety is normal following the devastation that can accompany the loss of a spouse. With that in mind:

1. Did you experience anxiety following the death of your spouse? If so, how did anxiety impact you?

_____

_____

_____

_____

_____

_____

_____

_____

_____

_____

2. What resources have you pursued in addressing the anxiety and/or depression? Which resources have been most helpful?

_____

_____

_____

_____

_____

_____

_____

_____

_____

_____

3. How is your self-care? Are there resources or additional actions you would like to take?

_____

_____

_____

_____

_____

_____

_____

_____

_____

# Chapter 4
### Sing When You Can't Understand
### by Nancy Honeytree Miller

As a Christian singer and songwriter, I have learned that singing to God, even when I don't understand what is happening in my life, allows me to regain perspective. I can better see who God is and lay my cares and concerns in His hands.

One day, years ago, as I was washing dishes, I prayed, "Lord, give me some encouragement to help me through this task." A song came to me, which I began to sing:

*I'm gonna believe that You are up to something good.*
*I'm gonna believe that You are up to something good.*
*When I can't understand the things that happen in my life,*
*I'm gonna believe that You are up to something good.*

*"I'll never fail or forsake you," that is what You said.*
*"Through fire and water I will take you," that is what You said.*
*So, when You don't answer my prayer the way I think You should,*
*I'm going to believe that You are up to something good.*[2]

That was a special day. My husband J.R. Miller and I hosted missionary guests, Ruth and Victor Martinez. They translated the song into Spanish and took it with them to the Centers of Faith, Hope, and Love in Mexico. There it became a favorite part of their worship!

When I wrote the song, it felt lighthearted. It was my way of expressing Romans 8:28, "And we know that in all things God works for the good of those who love Him, who have been called according to His purpose." But it stuck in my mind and stayed deep in my memory. Years later, when I experienced a tremendous crisis, this little song took on profound meaning and helped me to proclaim my faith in God's Word. Singing it was especially encouraging when I couldn't imagine how God

---

2      https://www.youtube.com/watch?v=Dq5ptVojRKU

could make something good out of my tragedy.

A year after I wrote "Up to Something Good," J.R. and I were expecting a baby. We had been married for four years. My pregnancy seemed to be going well, but in the fifth month, we were horribly stunned by tests results. Our baby boy was not expected to live. He had a triple 18$^{th}$ chromosome, a condition which causes severe birth defects.

J.R. and I were already in love with our son. The news of his condition broke our hearts and sent us into shock and tears. A day or two after receiving this devastating diagnosis, Ruth phoned from Mexico. "Nancy! What is happening? I had such a strong sense that I needed to call you!" When I told her what the doctors had said, she didn't say a word. She began to sing slowly, and every word plunged deeply into my heart.

*I'm gonna believe that You are up to something good.*
*I'm gonna believe that You are up to something good.*
*When I can't understand the things that happen in my life,*
*I'm gonna believe that You are up to something good.*

Tears streamed down my face. I had written this little song the year before, but now I desperately needed to hear Ruth sing it to me!

There was no way that J.R. and I could understand what was happening, but we gripped the truth of the song that God was somehow up to something good.

Little J.R. was born, then went to be with the Lord after just two hours. We were devastated, but the intense presence of Jesus made the short time with our baby sweet and precious.

But that wasn't the end of the story.

Two weeks before Little J.R. died, my doctor called to say that a baby would be available to adopt in about three months. We agreed to adopt him! In preparation, I pumped breast milk until baby William was born. Then I was able to breastfeed our adopted baby! Indeed, God was up to something good!

J.R. and I enjoyed raising our boy Will. He was friendly, strong, athletic, and funny. Our lives were full of the rich experiences of parenthood. It was also a challenge to raise Will because he was strong-willed and quick-tempered.

By the time Will was 22, J.R. was dealing with congestive heart failure. Even so, my husband was thriving, working full time, helping many ministries with their technology needs, and planning to retire and preach the Gospel. Though his body was struggling, his mind was focused on living. But on a Tuesday in May, J.R. suffered a heart attack and went to be with the Lord.

I had experienced grief when Little J.R. died, but the agony of losing my husband was unlike anything I had ever encountered. I felt alone and disconnected from the world around me. I felt like a fever radiated through my bones. It was as if J.R. and I had both gone down in a plane crash. He had died and I had walked away, traumatized.

When J.R. died, I was 66 years old. I had been a Christian for nearly 50 years. My mature relationship with the Lord helped me handle the many emotions and effects of my grief. I joined a GriefShare support group at my church and learned many helpful things about the grief process.

> *I realized the Lord was with me in my emotional highs and lows and everywhere in between!*

I wished that my Shepherd Jesus and I could just peacefully walk through the Valley of the Shadow of Death. But I was forced to also deal with Will's unexpectedly turbulent experience of grief. Will was not yet a mature adult when his dad died. He had not developed a strong walk with the Lord. He reacted with anger and participated in risky behavior to numb his feelings. Drinking alcohol and smoking marijuana led to relational problems with his wife, friends, employers, and me.

One day, while reading my Bible, I recognized that I had been drawn into Will's roller coaster ride of emotions. Psalm 139:7-8 says, "Where can I go from Your Spirit? Where can I flee from Your presence? If I go up to the heavens, You are there; if I make my bed in the depths, You are there." I realized the Lord was with me through my emotional highs and lows and everywhere in between! It was during this stormy time that God taught me to sing when I couldn't understand what was happening.

The Lord showed me that my emotional low points were often connected to bad news regarding Will's behavior. Indeed, I lived in a nervous state, dreading his next drama. "Again, son? Now what?"

I also felt a deep resentment toward the Lord, wondering "Why are You asking me to deal with such a nightmare when I feel so weak?"

I could not control my son's chaotic grief journey. But the Holy Spirit taught me to:

- pause and recognize when I was distressed,
- honestly admit my feelings and emotional anguish to Him, and
- sing to Him who is always worthy to be praised.

I would sing:

*Lord, I worship You.*
*You are worthy.*
*I sing Your praise.*
*You are on the throne of my life.*

As a new widow, weakened by grief, Will's issues piled drama on top of trauma! After a time of worship and prayer, I acquired a heavenly perspective and was able to put my son in the Lord's hands. My trust in the Lord's love for Will deepened, and I began to see him making progress in his healing. Will had a rough time but learned to make better decisions. And singing to God helped me to survive!

I discovered that there is spiritual power in singing! Psalms, the songbook of the Bible, says, "Sing to Him a new song" (Psalm 33:3). In the Old Testament story of Jehoshaphat, the singers were sent out in front of the army. When they sang, "Give thanks to the Lord, for His love endures forever," the enemies were so confused that they destroyed each other (2 Chronicles 20: 21-23). In the New Testament, we are told that Paul and Silas sang praises to God while they were in prison. A great earthquake shook the whole place so much that the prison doors flew open, and everyone's chains came loose. The jailer gave his heart to the Lord (Acts 16:25-33). Singing praise to God unleashed His power!

The Bible is full of references to singing. A favorite passage which has inspired many songwriters is Isaiah 6. King Uzziah had died and Isaiah the prophet was grieving. During this painful time, he saw the Lord high and lifted up with His glory filling the temple. The angels were worshipping around the throne! He said, "Woe is me!" In other words, he honestly recognized and verbalized his desperate state of unworthiness and need before the Lord. In that heavenly atmosphere, Isaiah was forgiven and cleansed. Suddenly he could hear the Lord asking, "Whom shall I send? Who will go for Us?" Isaiah responded, "Here I am, send me!" Worship empowered Isaiah. He went from "woe" to "go"!

This passage inspired me to write the song, "I See the Lord."

I see the Lord, high and lifted up,
Seated on the throne of my life.
And He is holy, He is holy,
He is holy, seated on the throne of my life. [3]

I learned that singing was also good for my health. As Harvard researchers state in Harvard Health Publishing, singing improves the immune system, brightens mood, increases energy, exercises lungs, stimulates circulation, releases muscle tension, and causes us to take in more oxygen.[4] No wonder the Lord encourages us to sing! He created singing to bring glory to Himself and healing to us!

I encourage you to decide today to worship God whether your emotions are high or low. Singing to the Lord will help you through the grief process. In doing so, you will be lifted into His glorious presence. You will find new strength for your journey.

---

3        https://www.youtube.com/watch?v=FI8LNihrWcc

4        https://www.health.harvard.edu/newsletter.article/In_Brief_Sing_along_ for_health. 9-4-21, 11:17 A.M.

# Questions for discussion:

1. Do you have a family member who is grieving in a destructive way? Releasing that person into God's hands will give you a heavenly perspective and help them progress in their healing.

_____

_____

_____

_____

_____

_____

_____

_____

2. In what ways are you experiencing drama on top of trauma?

_____

_____

_____

_____

_____

_____

_____

_____

3. Please take a few moments to ask the Holy Spirit to remind you to sing to Jesus and declare His worthiness, whether you are up or down.

_____

_____

_____

_____

_____

_____

_____

_____

_____

_____

4. When you are feeling low, consider the following steps:
   - Pause and recognize your feelings of distress,
   - Honestly admit your feelings to God, and
   - Sing to God regardless of your emotions.

_____

_____

_____

_____

_____

_____

_____

_____

# Chapter 5
*Pray, Pray, Pray!*
*by Chaplain Roberta Reyna, MA*

*Rejoice always, pray continually, give thanks in all*
*circumstances; for this is God's will for you in Christ Jesus.*
*I Thessalonians 5:16-18*

My relationship with God, through prayer, has been the foundation of my life. In every season, He has heard my cries for help. While He hasn't always responded in the way that I wished, He has always known what is best for me.

When I was eight years old, I understood the Gospel—that Jesus Christ died and rose again for my sins. I asked Him to forgive my sins and to become my Lord and Savior. This changed my life and the way I looked at everything around me. Before that, I tried to understand the reasons behind the circumstances. After that, I trusted God to teach me and guide me through life's adventures.

From the beginning of our relationship, I knew God as my best friend. He loved me with all His heart. His friendship has proven to be better than any earthly friendship.

As a child, I spent hours alone with Him, talking to Him, singing to Him, and listening to His sweet, loving, and sometimes authoritative voice. Each day, I read His Word over and over because I wanted to learn more about Him and become closer to Him.

Like everyone else, as I grew to adulthood, I experienced temptations, disillusionments, and difficulties, but He was always by my side. At times I would drift, but when I came back, He was always there with outstretched arms.

I married at age 23. During our 29 years of marriage, I had many difficult and bitter experiences. But in every situation, I went to God in prayer. He was my Comforter and my Provider.

As I matured in my relationship with God, I began to understand what the Bible means in I Thessalonians 5:17 where it says to pray continually. I learned that my relationship with God was a daily walk with Him. In order to maintain that harmonious relationship, I learned to practice these daily disciplines:

- To yield the authority over every area of my life to the lordship of Jesus Christ.
    - "Therefore, God exalted Him to the highest place and gave Him the name that is above every name, that at the name of Jesus every knee should bow, in heaven and in earth, and every tongue acknowledge that Jesus Christ is Lord to the glory of God the Father" (Philippians 2:9-11).
- To believe that all good things come from Him and work together for the good of those who love Him.
    - "Every good and perfect gift is from above, coming down from the Father of the heavenly lights, who does not change like shifting shadows" (James 1:17).
    - "And we know that in all things God works for the good of those who love Him, who have been called according to His purpose" (Romans 8:28).
    - "If you, then, though you are evil, know how to give good gifts to your children, how much more will your Father in heaven give good gifts to those who ask Him?" (Matthew 7:11).
    - "The Lord is good to those whose hope is in Him, to the one who seeks Him" (Lamentations 3:25).
- To believe that He is faithful and true to His Word. He will never lie.
    - "God is not a man, that he should lie, nor a son of man, that He should change his mind. Does He speak and then not act? Does He promise and not fulfill?" (Numbers 23:19).
    - "Let us hold unswervingly to the hope we profess, for He who promised is faithful" (Hebrews 10:23).
- To believe that as I humble myself and am willing to admit my sins and failures, I can rely on His great mercy and goodness as He accepts me and forgives all my

transgressions.

- "If we confess our sins, He is faithful and just and will forgive us our sins and purify us from all unrighteousness" (I John 1:9).
- "Because of the Lord's great love we are not consumed, for His compassions never fail. They are new every morning; great is Your faithfulness. I say to myself, 'the Lord is my portion; therefore, I will wait for Him'" (Lamentations 3:22-24).

- To worship Him, making it a habit to be thankful for who He is and who I am in Him. He is pleased when I show Him my appreciation by telling Him how good and great He is.

  - "Holy, Holy, Holy is the Lord God Almighty, Who was, and is, and is to come" (Revelation 4:8).
  - "You are worthy, our Lord and God, to receive glory and honor and power, for You created all things, and by Your will they were created and have their being" (Revelation 4:11).

- To consult Him before making decisions. He is all-knowing and always wants what is best for me. If I don't follow His plan, our relationship will suffer. I will experience adverse consequences because I departed from His path, which would have led me to blessings and abundant life.

  - "Your Word is a lamp for my feet and a light for my path" (Psalm 119:105).
  - "If you love Me, you will obey what I command" (John 14:15).

Because of these spiritual disciplines, I knew where to turn in the face of bad news. My husband had been sick for two years. After watching his health decline, he was finally diagnosed with incurable, metastatic cancer of the lung. I felt that I was in a dark pit, but I quickly sought my dear and faithful Friend to help me in my distress.

God allowed me to experience the truth that I was weak. Only as I leaned upon and trusted in Him could I become strong. I could not, through my own strength, produce joy, peace, health, provision, or anything else. These gifts only come from God, the Giver of all good things. As I went to Him in prayer, He blessed me with peace, security, joy, and hope. Every time I took my pain and sadness to Him, He wrapped me in His love and said, "Read my Word; believe in Me." He was my Comfort.

> My relationship with God, through prayer, has been the foundation of my life. In every season, He has heard my cries for help. While He hasn't always responded in the way that I wished, He has always known what it best for me.

I was 52 years old when my husband went to be the with the Lord. I had been a Christian for almost 44 years but still had much to learn about a life of prayer. At the time of this writing, I am almost 72 years old. I am still learning about prayer from the greatest Teacher of all time! He still often says, "Come to Me, all you who are weary and burdened, and I will give you rest" (Matthew 11:28).

It is vitally important that I listen to His voice. He is the Way, the Truth, and the Life (John 14:6). The solutions for my physical, emotional, and spiritual problems are found in Christ, through my faithful communication with Him. I don't need to pray eloquent words; I only need to pour out my heart to Him, and He will listen. I also need to listen to Him as I read and obey His Word.

After my husband's passing, I was responsible for huge medical bills, including charges for the hospital, doctors, and ambulance services. I cried as I thought about all the bills which were accumulating—my mortgage, utility bills, insurance, and car payments. Add to that a huge medical bill, and I would never be able to pay it all!

I went to the hospital Social Services office and pled with them to reduce my bill. They very coldly told me there was nothing they could do. I went back four more times, to no avail. Then I turned to the Lord. I cried and complained to Him, and He listened patiently. Then one day, I quit crying and asked the Lord what I could do about it. He reminded me of Jesus' parable in Luke 18:2-8:

In a certain town there was a judge who neither feared God nor cared about men. And there was a widow in that town who kept coming to him with the plea, 'Grant me justice against my adversary.'

For some time, he refused. But finally, he said to himself, "Even though I don't fear God or care about men, yet because this widow keeps bothering me, I will see that she gets justice, so that she won't eventually wear me out with her coming!"

Jesus was teaching his disciples to not give up. I realized that He was also telling me not to give up.

For the next three months, I continued going to the Social Services office, two or three times a week. When they saw me coming, I'm sure they wanted to run. However, the offices were arranged in such a way that they could not leave without going past me!

They continued to say that they couldn't help me. But I kept suggesting that they consider different options. Then a miracle happened! After persistently praying every day, I went one more time to the Social Services office. They explained that they had found a loophole! They could write off 80% of my bill, because my youngest daughter was under 18 years of age. I didn't understand why that made a difference, but I really didn't care! I was just concerned about paying my bill, and the Lord had made it possible for me to do so. Though I thought God was taking too long to answer my prayers, I discovered that His answer came just in time.

A few months after my husband died, I let a close family member stay in our home. They allowed another family member into my home who stole some of my checks. Without my knowledge, they wrote and cashed several large checks. I was so busy working, pastoring, and spending time with my two teenage daughters that I didn't realize what had happened. Two months later, I began getting late notices and charges from the bank for bad checks. My account was overdrawn by $10,000!

I was advised to file charges and send the thief to jail. But because it was a close family member, I didn't want to do that. I was very angry! So I went to my best friend, Jesus, and asked

Him what to do. He urged me to forgive them. Though I didn't really want to at first, I did comply with His command. Then I realized that if this person went to jail, they would have no way to make money to pay me back, anyway. So, I decided to confront them and leave it in God's hands. People told me I was crazy, but God told me to rest in Him.

It wasn't long before I had paid off all that I owed and had peace in my family. In the end, God brought calm to what had seemed like a catastrophe. I had a sense of joy and satisfaction, knowing I had obeyed the Lord and He had come to my rescue. He helped me in these hard financial situations.

God also answered my prayers for protection. Before going to work every day, I prayed that God would protect my daughters and my home. One day, I came home from work to find the front door open and the microwave oven on the floor. I immediately saw that someone had been there taking all the valuables. They had searched through the rooms and made a mess! They pulled out drawers and threw things on the floor. The TV, tape player, and many other things were gone!

I called the police and the insurance company. In less than a week, the insurance reimbursement check made it possible for me to purchase new appliances that were better than what I had before! I praised Him for turning a bad situation around for good.

After the burglary, my daughters and I no longer felt secure in the house. I prayed Psalm 34:7 over us: "The angel of the Lord encamps around those who fear Him, and He delivers them." I asked God to send His angels to camp around our home day and night. God answered my prayer and gave us peace.

I could continue to share so many situations where God has changed my circumstances and given me favor with other people! He truly has been a Faithful Friend, Companion, Protector, and Provider.

It has now been 20 years since my life was radically changed by my husband's passing. At the time, I felt a huge hole in my heart. My mind was full of doubts. I was faced with financial worries, guilt, and many other problems. I felt hurt, sad, alone, insecure, afraid, and without direction.

At that point, I made a wise decision. I turned to my Faithful Friend in prayer every time I was discouraged, depressed, or in need. As I prayed, prayed, prayed, He never failed to respond. He was always there—ready, willing, and able to help me. He taught me that prayer isn't just saying words—it is a continual, intimate conversation between two parties.

James 4:2 says, "You do not have, because you do not ask God." Many times, when I do not have what I need, it is because I haven't stopped long enough to talk to God about it. I might not even realize that I have not been communicating with Him regularly! When I talk to Him about my needs, He clarifies my perspective, supplies my needs abundantly, and gives me strength beyond my own.

As I walk with Jesus each day, I experience new joy. He is always with me in good times and bad. Everything I have and all that I am is a result of my intimate prayer times with the Lord. My strength, my health, and my well-being come from the One Who made us all and Who loves us more than anyone else.

If you'd also like to experience intimate relationship with God, I invite you to seek Him, and you will find Him. He is yearning to communicate with you. He wants to be your Strength, your Guide, your Protector, your Provider. He can be everything to you in this life and in the life to come. As you seek Him and learn to pray without ceasing, His blessings will become yours.

# Questions for Discussion:

1. Sometimes our communication with God comes through reading His Word. Have you heard God speak to you in this way? What did He say?

_____

_____

_____

_____

_____

_____

_____

_____

_____

_____

_____

_____

2. Sometimes our communication with God comes through prayer. How would you describe your current communication with the Lord?

_____

_____

_____

_____

_____

_____

_____

_____

_____

_____

_____

_____

_____

_____

3. What are some answers to prayer that you have experienced?

_____

_____

_____

_____

_____

_____

_____

_____

_____

_____

_____

_____

_____

_____

_____

# Chapter 6
*Caring for Yourself, the Widowed*
*by Linda Smith, BS*

Self-care is a very important subject to address after losing a spouse. If your marriage was anything like mine, you and your spouse probably took care of each other, to some extent. Now, self-care is your own responsibility. It's important to care for yourself not only for your sake, but also for your family and friends. Ignoring self-care can cause more problems later, so right now is the best time to begin. It's easier to stay out of a pit than to climb out once you have fallen into it.

Dear reader, you may have just suffered the greatest loss of your life. When you read this chapter, please give yourself lots of grace, especially if you are just beginning your grief journey. Maybe you can glean an idea or two that will help you move forward. Each step counts as a success. If you become overwhelmed, you might want to come back to this chapter later, or ask a friend to help you take care of yourself. Some of these ideas will be long-term goals, but some should be implemented as soon as you are able to gather enough courage and energy.

When I was first widowed, I gave myself a year of "kindness to self." I treated myself like I would treat a good friend. That worked so well, I decided to do it for another year. After two years, self-care became a habit!

I must make a disclaimer. I have been widowed for eight years, so I've been reconstructing my life for a while. I am not an expert in taking care of myself, so I will just tell you what has worked for me. This is more like a testimonial than a guidebook. If any of my ideas work for you, good. If they don't, please don't get stuck there. Ask around and find out what has worked for your other widowed friends.

Let's now look at taking care for our bodies, our responsibilities, and our opportunities.

There are obvious reasons for taking care of our bodies, but there are also spiritual reasons. Paul exhorts us:

Do you not know that your body is a temple of the Holy Spirit, Who is in you, Whom you have received from God? You are not your own, you were bought with a price. Therefore, honor God with your body (1 Corinthians 6:19-20).

Paul also says, "So we make it our goal to please Him, whether we are at home in the body or away from it" (2 Corinthians 5:9).

> *You may have just suffered the greatest loss of your life. When you read this chapter, please give yourself lots of grace, especially if you are just beginning your grief journey. Maybe you can glean an idea or two that will help you move forward. Each step counts as a success.*

So, your body is a tool for glorifying God, and your body belongs to Him. As you read the list below, consider the good habits that you already have and the ones you'd like to acquire:

- Eat well. It's not unusual to lose track of healthy eating if you are caring for a spouse who has been ill for a long time. My friend, Mary Beth, was hospitalized after her husband died because her iron levels had dropped to a life-threatening low during Bob's illness and passing. She was so intent on taking care of Bob, that she didn't take good care of herself. She became ill and didn't even realize it.

  Stress can also cause us to eat too many carbohydrates. We may not think ahead to plan meals. Fast food can also be a temptation when we have to eat alone. Because grieving seems to warp time, one can easily forget to eat. Loss of appetite is not uncommon but can be dangerous if it becomes habitual.

- Drink well. It's hard to drink too much water, especially if you are losing bodily fluid by crying a lot. An older woman once told me that not drinking enough water is like washing your clothes without detergent. Ew! Think about that. At home I have a 20-ounce water bottle that I need to fill—and drink—three times a day.

  Beverages other than water need to be consumed in

moderation. I love to drink coffee, but coffee is a diuretic, so I am working on reducing my coffee consumption and increasing my water intake. Drinking alcohol to deaden the pain of grief can be a trap. The Bible teaches moderation in all things, and it forbids drunkenness. That is not to spoil the party. That is wisdom inspired by God.

- Sleep well—or at least the best you can. Sometimes it's hard to sleep when you are suffering great loss. You might not even want to get into your bed alone. But sleep promotes healing, health, resilience, energy, memory and much, much more. Sleep also helps you grieve because your brain is problem-solving and processing memories while you sleep. Grief takes a lot of energy, so your body needs extra sleep. Prioritizing the time that you dedicate to sleep will serve you well.

  I watched my daughter sleep-train her babies. She would calm them down before bedtime. Then she put them in the same bed at the same time every night and woke them up at the same time every morning. Their first nap came at the same time every day. You get the idea. There was a rhythm that developed, and her babies thrived. They are older now, but they still have a time to go to bed and a time to get up. I think adults also benefit by putting themselves to bed at a regular time and getting up at a regular time. I have developed a rhythm for myself. As a result, I experience energy during the day and rest at night. My body knows when to sleep and when to wake. An added bonus is that I don't have to spend time trying to coax myself out of bed in the morning.

- Get some exercise. The benefits of exercise may not be obvious when you are grieving deeply, so start slowly. Begin with a short walk. You may enjoy exercise more by going outdoors. A side benefit of exercising outside is the Vitamin D which we get from sunshine. I love to meet up with a friend, especially if we go to the beach or to a hiking trail. As you get used to exercising, increase the length of time, the frequency, or the difficulty of your routine. Occasionally, I even reward myself by walking to a coffee shop or a store to buy a treat.

- Monitor your health. It is a good idea to visit your doctor within the first three months after the loss of your spouse. A professional assessment of your physical, mental, and emotional health will help you know how to plan your self-care. Your doctor might have other recommendations to help you survive this period of deep grief. Even putting a brighter, full-spectrum bulb in your lamp can help to dispel the darkness of soul by lighting up your room.

- Check your thoughts. Philippians 4:6-8 says:

  > Do not be anxious about anything, but in everything, by prayer and petition, with thanksgiving, present your requests to God. And the peace of God, which transcends all understanding, will guard your hearts and minds in Christ Jesus.

  > Finally, brothers, whatever is true, whatever is noble, whatever is right, whatever is pure, whatever is lovely, whatever is admirable—if anything is excellent or praiseworthy—think about such things.

  Paul is telling us that we need to guard our thinking and take our thoughts captive. We can help ourselves in this process by monitoring our exposure to stimuli. Personally, I have found that watching the news feeds anxiety, and God's Word relieves it. At any moment of the day or night, I can choose the focus of my thoughts.

- Pamper yourself. Proverbs 17:22 says, "A cheerful heart is good medicine, but a crushed spirit dries up the bones." Try to find something to do that you enjoy. Tinker in the workshop, paint some rocks, buy yourself a beautiful plant, take a mountain hike, re-watch a favorite old movie with a friend while sharing popcorn. Your grief won't vanish, but it may be a little more tolerable after you have enjoyed yourself.

Are there some ideas on this list that you are already doing? Keep doing them. Are there some that you could use to take better care of yourself? Write them down so you don't forget.

Now, let's turn our attention to the disorganization that naturally occurs after the loss of a spouse. In addition to our normal duties, we may inherit our late spouse's responsibilities.

This can feel overwhelming and chaotic. I would like to help you learn how to move from chaos to order.

When God created the earth, He brought order. He put the water over here and the land over there. The moon belongs in the sky, but not when the sun is there. Can you imagine The Trinity having a conversation about organizing creation?

God also organized the events that led up to the death and resurrection of Jesus—and our salvation! And think about the creation of a baby. Psalm 139 describes God's careful attention to every detail of the baby's development in the womb. In 1 Corinthians 14:33, Paul talks about order in the church. He says, "For God is not a God of disorder but of peace." This sounds like disorder is the opposite of peace. It certainly is for me.

One of my favorite tools for taming chaos is making lists. Because I'm a visual learner, I need to see the organizational pieces of my puzzle. If you have a hard time tracking tasks, a spiral notebook can keep all your lists in one place. I often have multiple lists—one for errands to run, another for household chores, another for money coming and going, etc. If you're a more random or kinesthetic learner, index cards or sticky notes might work better. That way, you can write down tasks and rearrange them.

When Kirby died, chaos ensued. Everything seemed to be spinning. There were so many things that needed to be done! My family and I made a list for funeral plans. We made another list of people bringing food. We made a list of tasks that needed to be done before more family arrived. We made a list of airport runs. I could not have organized these tasks without help from others. Grief gripped me with confusion and an inability to focus.

After we had composed our lists and determined dates and times for some items, we transferred those tasks to a calendar and crossed them off the lists. I call that "calendarizing." For example, "Call doctor" became a time and date on the calendar when I got an appointment. No more action was needed.

As we looked at the lists again, we decided that we should delegate some of these jobs. My sister would write the obituary and submit it to the newspaper. My daughter would be in charge of creating the video for the memorial service. We noted their names and then crossed the tasks off the lists because no more action was needed.

> $A$ s you gain skills in organizing, your confidence that you can indeed bring order out of chaos will grow.

In my new normal, I ended up hiring some help. I decided that it was not reasonable to add all of Kirby's tasks to my list. God provided workers I trusted, and the jobs got done. When we had delegated as many items from our lists as possible, we started to prioritize the tasks that were left. We numbered them in pencil so we could renumber them later. As time passed, I slowly regained my ability to manage my life.

As you gain skills in organizing, your confidence that you can indeed bring order out of chaos will grow. Here are just a few more miscellaneous tips:

- Sort your mail before you set it down.
  - Recycle the junk.
  - Put bills and letters that need a response in a rotating file by due date.
  - Put the condolence cards (happy mail) in a basket to read later.
- Get help with finances. If your spouse dealt with the taxes, investments, insurance, property titles, end-of-life documents, Social Security, etc., this is not the time for you to learn these new skills. I could not wrap my mind around these new concepts—at least not at the time. Sourcing it out has worked very well for me.
- When you are deciding which items to hire out, evaluate the fall-out if the job isn't done right. Your car needs an oil change to be done right because cars are expensive. Yardwork can usually be corrected without lasting consequences. I decided to pack my own boxes for moving because I had the time and energy, but I hired movers to carry all my stuff out to the truck and up to my third-floor condo. That took more strength than my friends or I had.

This new stage of life also offers new opportunities. One day, my husband came home from work and told us that he had just worked his last day at that job. His company had let him go. He would get severance pay for eleven months, and then he needed to be up and running, doing some other kind of work. This seemed like the end of the world, but in reality, it propelled Kirby to start his own business, which later proved to be a tremendous blessing.

Years later, I came home from the hospital where Kirby had just taken his last breath. I was no longer his wife; he would no longer be parenting our kids or grandkids. I would be able to collect life insurance, and then I would need to decide what to do next.

Kirby had accepted his challenge and started his own business. Would I also accept my challenge and move forward in God's plan for me? I took some time to contemplate my options and opportunities while I lived in the same house, went to the same church, and worked at the same job.

In Matthew 25 (NLT), Jesus tells us the parable about the man who entrusted his money to his servants and then left them. Two of the servants were resourceful and multiplied their master's money. The other servant replied, "I was afraid I would lose your money, so I hid it in the earth." The master was angry with the last servant's choice. Which servant would I choose to be like?

I have been afraid, to one degree or another, all my life. I have been afraid of failure. I have been afraid of new challenges. I have been afraid of disappointing others. I have been afraid of looking stupid. When Kirby died, I had to deal with my fears. I could bury them in the earth so no one would see them, or I could risk trying to learn new skills.

I found that in Proverbs 16:3 the Bible says, "Commit to the Lord whatever you do, and your plans will succeed." Isaiah 41:10 says, "So do not fear, for I am with you; do not be dismayed, for I am your God." As I was praying about this one day, the Lord said to me, "You still have thirty years left. Don't waste it." I am not a docile person, so something within me rebelled against the idea of sitting around for three decades playing Sudoku. That would make the enemy of my soul so happy and Lover of my soul, Jesus Christ, so disappointed in me. I decided then that I was going to risk some failures and lean into the opportunities that God brought my way.

I started small. My dad taught me how to change my furnace filter and use my power drill. I hired a crew to dig out my hedge and another crew to build a fence in its place. I learned how to book a flight, get to the airport, and find my luggage at the next airport. God helped me figure out some hard problems. I became confident of God's constant presence and communication with me. I eventually sold a house, bought a condo, and retired from my job. Yes, I had committed my plans to God. He made them succeed.

I mentioned Bible-reading and prayer. Both have been central to finding my way in this new chapter of my life. Galatians 4:4 says, "But when the time had fully come, God sent His Son, born of a woman, born under law." What law? On this earth, Jesus was subject to laws of nature such as gravity, pain, momentum, thirst, and cause and effect. Jesus demonstrated His priorities by spending time with His disciples. Communication was necessary.

In our relationships with Jesus, we are subject to that same law of cause and effect. If we spend little time with Jesus, we will know Him very little. If we spend lots of time with Him, we will know Him very well.

Jesus came to this earth with a purpose. It would have been so much easier for Him not to fulfill His purpose all the way to the cross, the grave, and then to Glory. I came to this chapter of my life with a purpose, and God is helping me deny my fears and find my purpose in Him. Jeremiah 29: 11-13 says:

> "For I know the plans I have for you," declares the Lord, "plans to prosper you and not to harm you, plans to give you hope and a future. Then you will call upon Me and come and pray to Me, and I will listen to you. You will seek Me and find Me when you seek Me with all your heart."

Jesus welcomes us to find Him in our grief.

This new chapter of life presents new challenges, responsibilities, and opportunities. Good self-care leads to better health which will enable us to find the physical, emotional, and spiritual strength to face the challenges of grief.

# Questions for Discussion:

1.  What ideas do you want to note here for taking better care
    of your body?

    _____

    _____

    _____

    _____

    _____

    _____

    _____

    _____

    _____

2.  Which area of your life would you like to organize first? Is
    there someone who could help you do that?

    _____

    _____

    _____

    _____

    _____

    _____

    _____

    _____

    _____

3. What opportunity/challenge in this new chapter of life strikes the most fear in you? Tell God all about it. Then write below what you think His response to you would be.

_____

_____

_____

_____

_____

_____

_____

_____

_____

_____

_____

# Chapter 7
*What Now? Finding Purpose In, During and After the Loss*
*by Ruth Martinez*

As of this writing, it has been two years since the passing of my beloved Victor. The pain I experienced from losing my husband of 48 years is indescribable. Only by God's grace have I been able to continue pressing forward.

Isaiah 41:10 says, "So do not fear, for I am with you; do not be dismayed, for I am your God. I will strengthen you and help you; I will uphold you with My righteous right hand." I can confidently say that God has been faithful to me. He has indeed sustained me with His righteous right hand, helped me, and accompanied me.

A verse that God brought to my mind the day my husband died was the same verse He gave my mother when she became a widow. "The Lord will fulfill His purpose for me; Your steadfast love, O Lord, endures forever. Do not forsake the work of Your hands" (Psalm 138:8 ESV).

At the same time, the words of Paul in 2 Corinthians 1:3-7 (Amplified Version) began to make sense to me:

> Blessed (gratefully praised and adored) be the God and Father of our Lord Jesus Christ, the Father of Mercies, and the God of all Comfort, Who comforts and encourages us in every trouble so that we will be able to comfort and encourage those who are in any kind of trouble, with the comfort with which we ourselves are comforted by God. For just as Christ's sufferings are ours in abundance (as they overflow to His followers), so also our comfort (our reassurance, our encouragement, our consolation) is abundant through Christ (it is truly more than enough to endure what we must). But if we are troubled and distressed, it is for your comfort and salvation; or if we are comforted and encouraged, it is for your comfort, which works (in you) when you patiently endure the same sufferings which we experience. And our hope for you (our confident expectation of good for you) is firmly grounded (assured and unshaken), since we

know that just as you share as partners in our sufferings, so also you share as partners in our comfort.

Before Victor died, we had already confirmed a three-month missionary trip, beginning two weeks after his passing. "What should I do?" I wondered. "Should I stay home and cry for three months? Or should I endeavor to comfort others while I am in the middle of grief?" My mind was blank. I had no sense of direction. The one who always prayed about and confirmed these invitations with me was no longer by my side.

My first question was, "How will I survive today? Will I be depressed, sad, in despair? Or could I possibly go through my "valley of tears" and emerge as a life-giving fountain? Will I continue to ask the 'why' question that has no answer this side of eternity? Or will I rise in the power of His love to fulfill my purpose in my new normal?"

I decided to go ahead and fulfill the commitments we had made. I asked my daughter Angela, a missionary in Nicaragua, to accompany me.

At our first Sunday service, we met a family of eight who had just lost their mother five days before. As we wept together for their loss, it brought a little comfort to my own soul, as well. During the following three months, I continued to preach and teach an average of once a day. In the process of ministering to other people, I began to realize that I was not the same person I had been when I was married to Victor. I would have to travel through this life without him, finding purpose and significance by myself.

> My life's purpose did not end when my beloved husband died. I have entered a new season of life, and I want to live it to the fullest, as I have in former seasons.

All this time, I was navigating the "valley of tears" without a map or a GPS. My sister Joy, also a widow, called me every day. My brother Mark called me from France. My children cried with me.

Then, I met Mary Beth Woll and Linda Smith, two widows

who were helping other widows. They led an online, 90-minute grief group. This weekly meeting of eight to ten widows provided a refuge in which we listened, understood, and cried together. One day, only the teachers and I showed up for class. That was my day! In this intimate setting, I was able to express my deep feelings of grief. They really listened and understood. That was a turning point for me.

There were two other decisive junctures in my grief journey. After I had been widowed for six months, I chose to pray, "Thank you, God, for my new life as a widow." At that moment, a very deep anguish was released from my soul.

I made a second critical decision at the one-year mark. Isaiah 61:3 says, God will "provide for those who grieve in Zion...a garment of praise instead of a spirit of despair." I realized I had been wearing what felt like a very heavy garment of sadness. I decided to take it off and receive God's garment of joy and happiness. As I walked through my valley of tears, God turned it into a place of springs. I claimed the faithful and true promises of God which assured me that nothing could separate me from His love. I cultivated an attitude of thankfulness and asked Him to give me a song in my heart every day.

I also learned that life in this world includes good news and bad news. John 16:33 says, "In this world you will have trouble." We will experience tears, pain, sorrow, sickness, tragedy, and death as long as we live in this fallen, sinful world. However, Jesus goes on to describe the good news: "Take heart! I have overcome the world." Eventually, as 1 Corinthians 15:26 says, "The last enemy to be destroyed is death."

Revelation 21:4 (NLT) says that one glorious day, "there will be no more death or sorrow or crying or pain." God Himself will wipe away every tear from our eyes. I can't wait for the day when God says, "Ruth, you don't need to cry anymore."

As a widow, I came to know the Holy Spirit in a new dimension, as the Comforter who would always be by my side. As Jesus promised:

But when the Helper (Comforter, Advocate, Intercessor— Counselor, Strengthener, Standby) comes, Whom I will send to you from the Father, that is the Spirit of Truth

Who comes from the Father, He will testify and bear witness about Me (John 15:26 Amplified).

What does it mean to be a comforter? A comforter relieves someone's pain or affliction. They bring help, consolation, and encouragement. They soothingly reassure, "Everything is going to be okay."

> *Reaching out to widows and orphans gave me new purpose in this stage of my life. I had a purpose as a single woman, and then as a wife. I have a purpose as a mother, a grandmother, and a great-grandmother. But now, I have a new purpose in my widowhood. I have decided to embrace this challenge and become a means of comfort to the grieving.*

Even as I began to experience relief from my own grief, I became aware that others around me were also suffering great loss. A pandemic sweeping Mexico claimed the lives of over 1,500 pastors. Nicaragua lost over 60 pastors. All of a sudden there was a flood of people who needed comfort. I reached out to comfort and weep with them. In one week alone, I called or messaged 50 new widows. I just had to do something to meet the needs of so many widowed and orphaned!

Sixteen months after my husband's passing, I instituted a weekly online outreach to ministry widows. We started with 30 but were soon flooded by a tsunami of requests from the widowed in all walks of life. Within five months, the project grew exponentially in Mexico and Central America. It became known as the "Legacy of Companionship." We were soon serving 700 widowed people.

Reaching out to widows and orphans gave me new purpose in this stage of my life. I had a purpose as a single woman, and then as a wife. I have a purpose as a mother, a grandmother, and a great-grandmother. But now, I have a new purpose in my widowhood. I have decided to embrace this challenge and become a means of comfort to the grieving.

Recently, I remodeled my home to become an oasis for ministry widows. I offer a retreat for five women at a time.

Often, I ask, "Precious one, how are you? How is your process going?" Sometimes I share a joke that Victor told. We recall how he encouraged others to be happy at all times. One thing leads to another. She shares about her late husband, we laugh and cry together, and soon one more person has been comforted.

I don't have to be strong and courageous. I only need to open my heart sincerely, which paves the way for another widow to receive healing. In this way, God allows me to alleviate the pain and affliction of someone else. I listen to them cry and walk alongside them in their grief journey. Others may avoid reaching out to the widowed because they don't know what to say. But by reaching out anyway, we learn when to speak and when to keep silent; when to hug or take their hand; and when to hold them as they sob. Because I have also suffered loss, I can journey with them and soothe their wounds.

I can do all this with tender, loving care because God gives me strength, stamina, and courage. He also gives me vision to see each step clearly. As I look back, I am not the same person I was 20 months ago when Victor died. With God's help, I have learned to make decisions and operate independently.

In the same way that I received comfort and consolation, I have now decided that I must give comfort and consolation to those who are grieving. My life's purpose did not end when my beloved husband died. I have entered a new season of life, and I want to live it to the fullest, as I have in former seasons. I could have been forever stuck with the "why" question. Instead, I decided to accept and even embrace my new normal while awakening to the urgent need to comfort others. My purpose is much greater than my pain.

Hebrews 10:24 encourages us to "spur one another on toward love and good deeds." I hope that my story will inspire you to find your own purpose after loss.

# Questions for Discussion:

1. Are there any "why" questions that are hindering you from finding your purpose?

   _____

   _____

   _____

   _____

   _____

   _____

   _____

   _____

   _____

2. Could you think of at least one person who has intentionally encouraged you?

   _____

   _____

   _____

   _____

   _____

   _____

   _____

   _____

   _____

3. Is there someone you could reach out to with the comfort you have received? When you do, Isaiah 61:2b (CEV) will become a reality: "The LORD has sent me to comfort those who mourn."

_____

_____

_____

_____

_____

_____

_____

_____

_____

_____

4. In what ways are you different now that your spouse has passed away?

_____

_____

_____

_____

_____

_____

_____

_____

_____

_____

5. What do you see as your purpose in this new season of your life?

_____

_____

_____

_____

_____

_____

_____

_____

_____

_____

# Chapter 8
*Rebuild*

*by Bruce McLeod*

Jesus said, "In this world you will have trouble. But take heart! I have overcome the world" (John 16:33). When I lost Cheri, it was certainly "trouble in this world" for me. When she died, I had anything but peace. Everything in my life was shattered, starting with my heart.

My emotions were intense and extremely varied. They ranged from guilt and shame to shock and sadness. I endured seasons of wordless howling like an animal, which left me confused and exhausted.

My mind was fragmented. I couldn't make sense of anything much. I couldn't grasp the meaning of more than a small page of print. As a voracious reader of deep things, I was extremely frustrated! My will—my "want to", I call it—was broken too. I just didn't want to do much but weep and sleep.

My health was broken. My sleep had been interrupted for months while I helped Cheri fight the cancer attack. Afterward, it all crashed in on me. Sleep apnea—which had not bothered me for years—returned with a vengeance. I suffered multiple, repetitive stress injuries to various parts of my body. I suffered two attacks of food poisoning that left my digestive system devastated.

All my life patterns changed overnight. Oh, how I longed for peace! I needed to rebuild my whole life and needed the Lord to show me how. I wanted to grieve in a healthy way. So, I needed to understand what my loss involved. He not only restored, but increased, my peace level. That took years to accomplish, but now it's greater than at any other time in my life. It's still in process. I've had to learn to curb my impatience. I'm trusting God, as never before, to do what only He can do.

Processing secondary losses was a major way God worked to bring me peace. Any loss has multiple levels. For example, my primary loss with Cheri was losing her person—who she was.

My secondary losses were all the roles Cheri played. In

our life together, Cheri was gardener, home decorator, and best friend. She was my lover, my business partner, and Chief Financial Officer of our businesses. I'm sure you get the idea. I wrote my own "lost-roles list" during my first time through the grief program. My list included forty-five different roles! Cheri was a lot to me! Today, only one role remains on the list. Jesus and I have dealt with the rest. They no longer grieve me. "My lover" is the one remaining role to grieve.

Processing secondary losses has facilitated my healing immensely. It has helped me understand who I am now that Cheri is gone. The following is the method I used to work through my secondary losses. In sharing my step-by-step program, I hope you too will find help and healing.

Take it slowly because it is a huge endeavor. If you try, and find it painful, please persevere. It will get easier. You could start by doing it with someone you trust. You could also do it in sections over time. Keep a journal to help you track your progress. Your primary loss is the person your spouse was. Cheri's name means "sweetheart." That's who she was for me—my "Sweet Heart." Begin your journal by describing who your spouse was for you. Then list your secondary losses. These are the roles your spouse played in your life together. They are things they did, not who they were. Write one loss as the heading for each page in your journal. Then record your impressions about each loss over time. Consider roles your spouse played in these areas:

- Roles for you personally (i.e., lover, hand-holder, date night partner)
- Roles in tasks and responsibilities (i.e., shopper, mechanic, bookkeeper, breadwinner)
- Roles in childcare or nurturing others (i.e., comforter, listener, calendar keeper, hostess)
- Roles played in your hopes and dreams for the future (i.e., travel companion, chief grandkid playmate, idea generator)

The list may change over time. You may add other categories as needed. The Holy Spirit will help you with this. He is very good at prompting grief work. I was hungry for His help, and my heart was completely open to Him. I was able to delete items as

I went along. I added some as well.

The next step is grieving aloud to God each secondary loss.

- Use as many words, and allow as many tears, as possible.
- When you have expressed yourself completely to God, ask Him for His comfort and counsel regarding that loss.
- Listen to Him and record any impressions you receive from Him.
- Date each entry.

Repeat this practice periodically until all your losses have been healed. In the beginning, I had to spread my grief sessions out over several days. It took hours to get through my whole list. I just couldn't do it all in one day. This was exhausting, so I didn't expect much of myself afterward. I might cook, do laundry, go shopping, or do other light work.

I calendared monthly grief appointments with God for over three years. That's how long it took for Jesus to heal forty-four secondary losses. It may take more or less time for you. It takes as long as it takes.

A beautiful setting, in which to meet God, also helped me move forward. God's creation speaks healing to my heart. Find a place that does that for you and meet with God there.

I'd like to share how I removed some of my secondary losses from my list:

- Chief Financial Officer: As I lamented this loss, I received this comfort from the Lord, "You don't need a CFO anymore, Bruce. Without Cheri, you own no businesses." Then came the counsel: "Cross it off your list." I did.
- Head Gardener: This one took several months to resolve. In this case, the counsel came first, "Hire some landscaping help. Plant vegetables next year, not now." Then came the comfort, "Cheri would understand. Remember, she was widowed when you met her. Cross it off." I did, after I

hired the landscaper.

- "The Baby Whisperer:" Cheri could comfort almost any crying baby, who would soon fall asleep in her arms. Again, first came the counsel: "There are no babies, or prospects of them in your family, Bruce. You don't need the Baby Whisperer anymore." Then came the comfort: "Cheri and I taught you to care for kids, Bruce. She gave you some of her sweet heart. You love your kids, grandkids, and the neighborhood kids. They know it and they love you. Cross it off." I did.

- Event Partner: This one took a while to resolve. Cheri and I used to work together to host dinners and sleepovers for our family. We also presented weekend seminars and hosted weekly groups. Together, we prepared for, facilitated, debriefed, and recovered from these events. We each had different responsibilities.

  After Cheri passed, I continued to host some events, myself. Over a period of three years, the Lord led me to go about it differently. I learned to spread out the preparation for an event over several days. I hosted events that did not require husband/wife co-facilitators. He taught me how to debrief my events with Him. He led me to take longer for cleanup and recovery. I found a "new normal" for my events. I crossed "Event Partner" off the list.

I pray that these examples will encourage you. I believe God used this practice to heal my broken heart. He fulfilled the Scripture promise quoted at the beginning of the lesson; amid deep trouble, He gave me peace. I believe He will do it for you too.

Another area that required rebuilding involved the first and second times I experienced significant days and dates. Because Cheri passed on the 14th of December, every 14th day of the month became a potential grief ambush. Likewise, our anniversary, her birthday, and the many holidays that we used to celebrate together could trigger grief. In the early days of grief, going to church could also be a trigger for me.

Here are some of the things I learned to do to weather these emotionally intense days:

- Plan ahead. Anticipate significant days and prepare in advance. Decide in which traditional activities you will participate and in which you won't. I didn't set up a Christmas tree that first year. I didn't go out to dinner to celebrate our anniversary until the fourth one after Cheri passed. I wanted to wait until I could celebrate Cheri's impact on my life.

- Expect less of yourself. On significant days, find ways to lighten your workload. You could schedule the day off from work. Buy a meal instead of cooking. Allow yourself to cry. Don't attempt to do everything you and your spouse did together.

- Arrange for company. Don't spend the whole day alone. Visit or call a sympathetic family member or friend. Make reservations to share a meal at a restaurant. Arrange in advance to sit with friends at church.

- Plan your escape. When you are away from home, prepare a way to leave gracefully, should you need to. I learned to ask hosts if I could come late and leave early. I used to sit near an exit door when I went to church. Where possible, identify a place in the building where you can be alone for a few minutes if you need to calm yourself.

- Recognize the effects of emotional shock. Grief experts tell us that being widowed numbs us emotionally for the first six to nine months. We just don't feel as deeply as we used to—or will. As the numbing effect wears off, some people may experience their pain more deeply in the second year. My first Christmas arrived just ten days after Cheri died. It was a blur. I don't remember much at all about it. By the time the second Christmas arrived, the numbness was gone. I felt awful! I really fell apart. The same was true of Valentine's Day, Easter, our wedding anniversary, and Cheri's birthday. Knowledge is power! So, I learned to anticipate and prepare for these important dates.

- Stay on guard. Even after I implemented my plan for special days, I sometimes still experienced grief ambushes. Often enough, my plan for the day worked well. However, I was unprepared for grief attacks that came before or after the special day itself. I call the latter "the let-down effect." Irrational fear sometimes caused me anxiety before the special day. All of these are normal grief experiences.

As I have implemented these practices, I have experienced more peace. Holidays and anniversaries are once again becoming celebrations instead of terrors. Tears of joy for the life Cheri and I shared have replaced the tears of pain and sadness.

I pray these tools will help you. Our old life is gone. It will never come again. However, together with God, our Creator, we can construct a great and joyful new life. He promises to do more in each of us than we can ask or even imagine.

1 Peter 5:6-11 (MSG) says:

So be content with who you are, and don't put on airs. God's strong hand is on you; He'll promote you at the right time. Live carefree before God; He is most careful with you. Keep a cool head. Stay alert. The devil is poised to pounce and would like nothing better than to catch you napping. Keep your guard up. You're not the only ones plunged into these hard times. It's the same with Christians all over the world. So, keep a firm grip on the faith. The suffering won't last forever. It won't be long before this generous God who has great plans for us in Christ—eternal and glorious plans they are!—will have you put together and on your feet for good. He gets the last word; yes, He does.

# Questions for Discussion:

1.  What are some of the secondary losses you have experienced?

    _____

    _____

    _____

    _____

    _____

    _____

    _____

    _____

2.  How might processing secondary losses look for you? Where
    would you do it? When and how often?

    _____

    _____

    _____

    _____

    _____

    _____

    _____

    _____

    _____

3.  What are some "firsts" and anniversaries that could be hard
    for you? Make a written list.

    _____

    _____

    _____

    _____

    _____

    _____

    _____

    _____

    _____

    _____


4.  How will you successfully get through those emotionally
    charged days? Which of the suggestions offered in the
    chapter do you want to try?

    _____

    _____

    _____

    _____

    _____

    _____

    _____

    _____

    _____

# Chapter 9
*Moving Forward*
*By Linda Smith, BS*

After 37 years of marriage, I suddenly found myself single. Though Kirby had been ill for several years, I was jolted by the aftershocks of his passing. I needed to hear from God about navigating this new, solo lifestyle. When Kirby and I were married, I knew his favorite colors, how to finish some of his sentences, or where he would like to spend a sunny, summer evening. I needed to know God like that—His voice, His purposes, and His actions. I needed to know Him who is the Way, the Truth, and the Life (John 14:6).

When Kirby died, I could no longer depend on him to take care of me or to seek God for me. I had to learn to seek Him for myself and to take care of myself spiritually. At first, this seemed like a daunting task—too hard to wrap my mind around. But I needed to find out what God had in mind for me.

I was suddenly in a new chapter of my life, but God's Word assured me, "You did not choose Me, but I chose you and appointed you to go and bear fruit, fruit that will last" (John 15:16). I still had a purpose for living. I was God's beloved, chosen daughter. I trusted my heavenly Father and His plan for me.

I wrote Jesus a letter:

> I worship You. Help me to make choices that honor and glorify You—choices that draw me close to You. I love You. I worship You. I want to live the rest of my life in complete surrender to You. I pray that I will always have attentive ears and a willing heart. Lead me and guide me every day, I pray.
> Thank You, Jesus.
> Love,
> Linda

Years earlier, in another time of crisis, God had alleviated my fears with the following Scripture. After Kirby died, I clung to it for dear life:

His divine power has given us everything we need for life and godliness through our knowledge of Him who called us by His own glory and goodness. Through these He has given us His great and precious promises, so through them you may participate in the divine nature and escape the corruption of the world caused by evil desires. For this very reason, make every effort to add to your faith goodness; and to goodness, knowledge; and to knowledge, self-control; and to self-control, perseverance; and to perseverance, godliness; and to godliness, brotherly kindness; and to brotherly kindness, love. For if you possess these qualities in increasing measure, they will keep you from being ineffective and unproductive in your knowledge of our Lord Jesus Christ (2 Peter 2:3-8).

I wondered what those great and precious promises were, so I began searching my Bible.

- Psalm 23 says He guides me, supplies my needs, restores my soul, takes away my fears, is with me even in the "Valley of the Shadow of Death." Goodness and love will follow me. He anoints me and protects me. What awesome promises!

- Philippians 2:13: "It is God who works in you to will and to act in order to fulfill His good purpose." He's willing to show me His purposes!

- Philippians 4:7 promises us: "The peace of God which transcends all understanding, will guard your hearts and your minds in Christ Jesus." Oh, I wanted that! Verse 6 tells us how to get it. "Do not be anxious about anything, but in everything, by prayer and petition, with thanksgiving, present your requests to God."

- Matthew 6:33-34 says this about worrying: "But seek first His Kingdom and His righteousness, and all these things will be given to you as well. Therefore, do not worry about tomorrow, for tomorrow will worry about itself. Each day has enough trouble of its own."

Every day looked like a mountain too tall to climb, but these promises brought me great comfort—and challenge! It sounded like I had to do my part too. I prayed. I was feeling so tired and sad, but as I considered 2 Peter 1: 8, I felt scared at the thought of being "ineffective and unproductive." I did not want those words in my obituary. I wanted "good and faithful servant" to describe me (Matthew 25:23). As I prayed about the "how" and "what" of my future, God spoke to me. He said, "Linda, you have 30 years left to live. That is a lot of time. Don't waste it!"

Thirty years would be a long time to sit in my rocking chair, playing Sudoku and feeling sad about being a widow! A rebellion against the enemy of my soul rose up within me. I didn't know "how" or "what" yet, but I was not going to waste the rest of my life.

> *I still had a purpose for living. I was God's beloved, chosen daughter. I trusted my heavenly Father and His plan for me.*

I did not make any big changes at first. I was too frazzled by my loss and the new responsibilities that went with it. I kept going to work, worshipping with my church family, and living in the same house. I pursued closer communication with God. He was now my Husband—my Protector, Provider, Leader, and Guide. Four weeks after Kirby died, I had to have open-heart surgery. My parents came to take care of me physically, mentally, and spiritually. (They had also been with me when Kirby died.) This provided me time off work and time to seek the Lord.

As I pondered my new commitment to God, I ran across this in Henry Blackaby's "Knowing and Doing the Will of God" (Blackaby, p. 12):

- Agree that God is absolutely trustworthy.
- Agree with God that you will follow Him one day at a time.
- Agree that you will follow Him even when He does not spell out all the details.
- Agree that you will let Him be your WAY. [5]

Slowly but surely, God's plan began to emerge. He was

5    Experiencing God, Knowing and Doing the Will of God, Henry T. Blackaby and Claude V. King, Lifeway Press, Nashville, TN, 1997, p. 12.

preparing me to live His way. I began to think about my house and how sustainable it would be for me to stay there. I tried renting out bedrooms but decided I preferred to live alone.

I began to realize how much time, energy, and money my house maintenance required. I hired help to mow the lawn, paint the house, take out the hedge, install a fence, etc. I did a lot of the work myself. After I suffered a knee injury, I discovered how often I was used to running up and down the steps. I concluded that I could not grow old in this house. God was preparing me for change.

Circumstances at work were making me want to retire. I thought age 65 seemed like a nice, round number, but there were too many transitions already happening at work. The other person in my office was leaving, so I continued to pray about when I would retire. I trusted God to choose just the right time for me.

In Blackaby's book he says that God speaks to us in various ways:

1.  God speaks through the Bible.

    - Psalm 119:105: "Your Word is a lamp to my feet and a light for my path."
    - Psalm 19:7-8: "The law of the Lord is perfect, reviving the soul. The statutes of the Lord are trustworthy, making wise the simple. The precepts of the Lord are right, giving joy to the heart. The commands of the Lord are radiant, giving light to the eyes."

    The Bible is so full of guidance for our everyday lives and for specific problems!

2.  God speaks through the Holy Spirit, the Spirit of Truth.

    - John 14:16: "And I will ask the Father, and He will give you another Counselor to be with you forever—the Spirit of Truth."

    Relationship with God activates the work of the Holy Spirit in our lives.

3.  God speaks through prayer.

    - Romans 8:26-27: "In the same way, the Spirit helps us in

our weakness. We do not know what we ought to pray for, but the Spirit Himself intercedes for us with groans that words cannot express. And He who searches our hearts knows the mind of the Spirit, because the Spirit intercedes for the saints in accordance with God's will."

Intimacy with God leads to watching and waiting and asking God to move.

4. God works through your circumstances.

- In John 6:1-15, Philip could only see 5,000 hungry men with their families, and a boy with five loaves and two fish. But Jesus could see God's ample provision for the crowd, with leftovers!

God's perspective is different than ours because He sees the whole picture!

5. God works through His Church.

- I Corinthians 12:25: "...so that there should be no division in the Body, but that its parts should have equal concern for each other."

- Ephesians 4:15-16: "Instead, speaking the truth in love, we will in all things grow up into Him who is the Head, that is, Christ. From Him the whole body, joined and held together by every supporting ligament, grows, and builds itself up in love, as each part does its work."

His Body has people who can give us godly, wise advice, if we ask. Stay connected with God's people. God might speak to you through them.[6]

One Friday evening, as I was contemplating whether or not to sell my house, I asked my dinner guests to pray with me. We four attended the same church, and they cared very much about my decision. The next morning, my devotional said this: "When I give you no special guidance, stay where you are. Concentrate on doing your everyday tasks in awareness of My presence with you. Thus, you invite Me into every aspect of your life" (Jesus Calling, Sarah Young, p. 108). [7]

---

6    Experiencing God, Knowing and Doing the Will of God, Henry T. Blackaby and Claude V. King, Lifeway Press, Nashville, TN, 1997, p. 12.
7    Jesus Calling, Enjoying Peace in His Presence, Sarah Young, Thomas Nelson, Nashville, TN, 2012, p. 108

That was clearly an answer to our prayers. So, I waited and listened and watched and wondered. God was preparing me for change—but not yet.

I assessed my possessions and decided that I did not want to spend my retirement taking care of all that stuff. Surely, God must have something better for me! I needed to downsize and simplify. I started dealing with the big stuff first. I gave Kirby's car to my daughter and son-in-law. With the help of a lawyer, I dissolved Kirby's home business and began giving away his office furniture and equipment. He had 13 years-worth of paperwork in our basement that I needed to shred.

Then I needed to deal with his clothes. Kirby did not care much about fashion, so I tossed some of his clothes in the garbage with glee! I decided to keep a few of his clothes—at least for a while.

I invited my son and daughter to come and take whatever they wanted of their dad's possessions.

As I began to pare down our belongings, I asked myself several questions:

1. When did I last use this?
2. How soon might I use it again?
3. Would it be hard to replace this item if I needed it later?
4. Does it hold sentimental value?
5. Can I take a photo of it instead of keeping it?

We had lived in this house for 29 years and next-door for 13 years. You can imagine that I had a lot of work to do, and God gave me time to do it.

As I continued to pray about when to sell my house, the real estate taxes came due. Every year, taxes had increased at an alarming rate. As I did the math and projected into the future, I concluded that I could not afford to retire and live in this house. This was a pivotal moment. I was praying. God was speaking.

I told my family and a few others that I was planning to sell my house. Then came the questions: "Sell when?" "Live where?" "In a house or in a condo?" "Rent or buy?"

I began narrowing down my preferences. I made lists of pros and cons. I prayed, and I prayed. I decided that I wanted to buy a condo near my daughter and my church. I remember asking God how to even begin to find a new home. I was overwhelmed, but I prayed.

One day, my daughter told me that her mother-in-law's friend was planning to sell her nearby condo. I asked my daughter to give me her phone number. Within that week, her friend invited me to come and see her condo, which was just five miles from my daughter and a mile and a half from my church. It felt like home the minute I walked in the door. It was on the top floor, it was very private, and the space was laid out the way I would have designed it!

She asked me to sign a letter of intent to buy her condo. The Lord then helped me finance the purchase of the condo and hire a painter.

I also hired a helper to sell my stuff, take my stuff, and give my stuff away. I was frantically packing and downsizing. A co-worker recommended a moving company she had used six times, so I hired them to move my stuff. By then I was feeling like a Proverbs 31 woman: "She sets about her work vigorously; her arms are strong for her tasks" (v. 17). God was indeed giving me everything I needed to move forward into His plans for me.

I still needed to sell my house in Seattle, but I knew God would be with me in that task, too. It was easier to prepare my house for sale because I had already removed my belongings. God gave me strength, and friends helped me get my house ready.

My real estate agent recruited someone to stage my house. I thought the asking price was too low, but I felt impressed by God to not complain. I prayed, and I'm glad I did! The buyer paid 13.5% above the asking price. That must have been God's plan too!

God keeps giving me everything I need for living a godly life, through my knowledge of Him—just like He promised. I keep talking with Him along the way, and He keeps showing me what to do. I'm sure that as you seek God and His purposes first, He will give you everything you need, too. "You did not choose Me, but I chose you and appointed you to go and bear fruit, fruit that will last" (John 15:16). He keeps His promises!

Now that I was settled into my new home, it was the perfect

time to retire. I told my boss that I was planning to retire on my 66<sup>th</sup> birthday. And so, I did! That was perfect timing too—God's timing.

# Questions for Discussion:

1. Have you settled these issues in your heart? Can you:
   - Agree that God is absolutely trustworthy?
   - Agree with God that you will follow Him one day at a time?
   - Agree that you will follow Him even when He does not spell out all the details?
   - Agree that you will let Him be your WAY?

   _____

   _____

   _____

   _____

   _____

   _____

   _____

   _____

   _____

   _____

   _____

2. Which of God's promises are most dear to you?

   _____

   _____

   _____

_____

_____

_____

_____

_____

_____

_____

_____

_____

_____

_____

3. How is God speaking to you about your daily life and decisions?

_____

_____

_____

_____

_____

_____

_____

_____

_____

_____

_____

_____

_____

4. If you feel comfortable with it, take a few minutes to write a love letter to Jesus.

_____

_____

_____

_____

_____

_____

_____

_____

_____

_____

# Chapter 10
*Complicated Grief*
*By Mary Beth Woll. MA, LMHC*

Writing this chapter has been a challenge for me. It required some deep soul searching. I had been a therapist for 16 years. I had walked with the Lord all my life. I was educated in the Word of God. I was well-connected with family and friends. My life was extraordinarily rich and very blessed. And yet, I, too, suffered complicated grief after the loss of my husband Bob.

Those of you who have lost a spouse may be asking, "Isn't all grief complicated?"

Yes, in a sense, all grief is complicated and very messy. At the beginning of the grief process, we will likely experience disbelief, numbness, searching—sometimes even passing suicidal thoughts—as we long to be in the presence of our loved one.

And then, the disorganization begins. We can also experience symptoms in our body, soul, and spirit, such as desperate sadness, loneliness, and anxiety. These are all symptoms of a normal grief experience.

In his book, "A Grief Observed," C. S. Lewis wrote:

No one ever told me that grief felt so like fear. I am not afraid, but the sensation is like being afraid. The same fluttering in the stomach, the same restlessness, the yawning. I keep on swallowing. At other times it feels like being mildly drunk or concussed. There is a sort of invisible blanket between the world and me. I find it hard to take in what anyone says. Or perhaps, hard to want to take it in. It is so uninteresting. Yet I want the others to be about me. I dread the moments when the house is empty. If only they would talk to one another and not to me.

I also did not know that grief felt like fear. I was strong for Bob when he was in the hospital. Except for brief breaks, I was with him until the very moment he died. But as I entered the shock and then the disorganization phase of grief, I experienced tremendous physical symptoms as well as debilitating anxiety.

As my doctor explained, my body was responding to trauma as if I was running from a bear!

I went through the typical stages of shock and denial, anger, bargaining, depression, and finally acceptance. But because of the trauma of Bob's passing, and my temporary illness as a result of caregiving, I was dysfunctional for six months. It is only by a miracle of God and the help of family and friends that I did not get stuck in complicated grief. I leaned hard on the Lord and experienced what Psalm 34:18 says, "The Lord is close to the brokenhearted and saves those who are crushed in spirit."

> Complicated grief is when, in the process of letting go of what we can no longer keep, we get stuck in grief and are not able to move forward through these stages.

In a sense, every loss is traumatic because we are deprived of our loved one. According to the Merriam-Webster Dictionary, the word bereavement comes from an old English word meaning "to rob." So, if a typical grief process is painful, messy, and complex, what on earth is complicated grief?

Complicated grief is when, in the process of letting go of what we can no longer keep, we get stuck in grief and are not able to move forward.

Usually, after moving through shock and disorganization, we are gradually able to accept the reality of our loss and organize ourselves into a new life without our loved one. We need to be patient with ourselves during this painful time. We begin to cultivate connections with family and friends that fill the gap of that primary relationship. We may even choose to remarry. All these things are a normal part of grief. But, if a person is unable to make at least some forward movement within a year following the death of their loved one, they may be experiencing complicated grief.

Symptoms of complicated grief may include:

- Intense sorrow, pain, and rumination over the loss of the loved one
- Focusing on little else but the loved one's death

- Extreme focus on reminders of the loved one or excessive avoidance of reminders
- Intense or persistent longing or pining for the deceased
- Problems accepting the death
- Numbness or detachment
- Bitterness about the loss
- Feeling that life holds no meaning or purpose
- Lack of trust in others
- The inability to enjoy life or to think back on positive experiences with the loved one[8]

During the first few months after the loss of a loved one, we may all experience these symptoms. However, God designed the grief process to allow us to gradually let go of the past, and these symptoms do start to fade over time.

But sometimes, in the case of complicated grief, these symptoms linger, or even get worse. Complicated grief is like being in an ongoing, heightened state of mourning. Much like repeatedly pulling a scab off a wound, this keeps a person from healing.

The social aspects of complicated grief include:

- Trouble carrying out our normal routines
- Isolating from others and withdrawing from social activity
- Experiencing depression, deep sadness, guilt, or self-blame
- Believing that we may have done something wrong or could have prevented the death
- Feeling that life isn't worth living without our loved one
- Feeling that we wish we had died with our loved one (Mayo Clinic, 2021)

According to the Mayo Clinic, complicated grief occurs more often in females and with older age. Risk factors that increase

---

8       (mayoclinic.org, 10-08-21, 9:28 p.m.) https://www.mayoclinic.org/
diseases-conditions/complicated-grief/symptoms-causes/syc-20360374

the possibility of developing complicated grief may include:

- An unexpected or violent death, such as death from a car accident, or the murder or suicide of a loved one
- Close or dependent relationship to the deceased person
- Social isolation or loss of a support system or friendships
- Past history of depression, separation anxiety or post-traumatic stress disorder (PTSD)
- Traumatic childhood experiences, such as abuse or neglect
- Other major life stressors, such as major financial hardships
- Multiple losses
- Witnessing the loss or not being there when the loss occurred
- Losses due to medical errors or the neglect of caregivers
- A genetic predisposition to depression or anxiety
- A history of substance abuse (Mayo Clinic, 2021)

Treatment for complicated grief can include:

- Sharing: Sharing about your grief and allowing yourself to cry also can help prevent you from getting stuck in your sadness. In most cases, your pain will start to lift as you allow yourself to feel it and talk about it.
- Support: Family members, friends, social support groups and your faith community are all good options to help you work through your grief. You may be able to find a support group, such as The Widows Project, that focuses specifically on the loss of a spouse.
- Bereavement counseling: Through early counseling after a loss, you can explore your emotions and learn healthy coping skills. This may help prevent negative thoughts and beliefs from gaining such a stronghold that they are difficult to overcome.

At The Widows Project, we've discovered that people need to tell their story—usually over and over again. As we tell our story to God and safe people, the trauma—like black paint in a watercolor—begins to blend into the canvas of our lives as a critical part of who we are becoming.

Those of us who have lost a spouse understand the need to repeat our grief story. But others who have not suffered a similar loss may urge us to "stop talking and move on." This attitude is not for the benefit of the grieving person, but to ease the discomfort of the listener who does not understand the grief process. In fact, the exact opposite is true! As we tell our story to safe people, our brains begin to heal. We can begin to tell ourselves: "That trauma is not really happening now. I'm safe now. My loved one is safe in the arms of Jesus. Now, I can begin to take steps to move forward."

Bereavement counseling can take many forms, but the goal is to resolve the complicating event or trauma so that the grieving person can move forward toward the acceptance of their loss. Then they can begin building a new life without their loved one.

Some people say, "Time heals all wounds." This is not the case with complicated grief. As Henry Cloud states in his book "Changes that Heal," it is only "good time" that heals. "Good time is time in which we and our experiences can be affected by grace and truth. Grace and truth cannot affect the part of ourselves we won't bring into experience." [9]

Over a period of time, we can grow and heal from complicated grief if we are able to:

- Tell our story,
- Receive support such as grace and truth from God and the Body of Christ and, if necessary,
- Pursue counseling.

Complicated grief has many causes and symptoms. Sometimes the person experiencing these symptoms is not aware that their grief has become complicated. It's important for their family and friends to recognize that they are not progressing through the typical stages of grief. They may need assistance in getting the help that they need.

---

9      Changes That Heal, Dr. Henry Cloud, Zondervan Publishing House, Grand Rapids, MI, 1992, p. 37

# Discussion Questions:

1. C. S. Lewis described a sort of invisible blanket between the world and himself. Did you experience anything like that?

_____

_____

_____

_____

_____

_____

_____

_____

_____

_____

_____

2. In what ways can grief feel like fear?

_____

_____

_____

_____

_____

_____

_____

_____

_____

_____

_____

_____

3. A year after their loss, some people may consistently feel the pain as acutely as they did the day their spouse died. This is complicated grief. Have you, or someone you know, experienced this?

_____

_____

_____

_____

_____

_____

_____

_____

_____

_____

_____

_____

_____

_____

# Chapter 11
*Widowed Parenting: Tips for Parenting after Loss*
*by Lisa C. Greene, M.A., CFLE*

One can never be prepared for the words, "I am sorry, but your husband has passed." That certainly was my experience when my husband unexpectedly died from a heart attack. The shock, numbness and eventual flood of emotions felt like a rollercoaster. One minute I was a walking zombie, unable to remember even the simplest things like how to get to the grocery store. The next minute I was pulling off to the side of the road for an uncontrollable flood of tears. As you have already read in previous chapters, this is normal.

The shortest verse in the Bible is "Jesus wept" (John 11:35). Even Jesus grieved when his dear friend Lazarus died. Imagine that! The Lord of life and death wept at the earthly loss of his friend and at the pain and suffering of others around Him. Like Jesus, as you weep for yourself and your own loss, you are also grieving for your children. Your children are grieving, too. However, their grief may look different than yours. This, too, is normal.

My son and daughter were 16 and 14 when my husband suddenly passed. I remember being very surprised by their insistence to go to school the next day. I was in shock and barely able to function. I thought they would feel the same way. However, I had much to learn about how differently kids process grief than adults. Here are some of the things I have learned over the years since my husband passed away:

1.  The first, most important, and sometimes hardest thing to do is to take good care of yourself. You are now doing the work of two people in all aspects of life including parenting. Set aside time for yourself—even 5 minutes a day—so you don't put yourself at risk for health problems, such as depression and anxiety. Taking care of yourself sets a good example for your children. You are modeling self-care. So, take a guilt-free moment for yourself. You need it! You deserve it!

2.  Kids process loss much differently than adults do. They

may cry, be angry, or withdraw. However, it is also normal for them to appear unaffected and want to get right back to their lives. They may even joke around in seemingly inappropriate ways. Each child is different and will process their grief based on their personality, life experiences, previous losses, and cultural influences. That being said, it's important to offer your child opportunities to actively grieve. Here are some tips:

- Be honest with your children about the circumstances of your spouse's passing. Understandably, adults want to try and protect children from harsh realities. The problem is that children perceive a lot more than we realize. While they may not be able to handle every medical detail, it is important to tell them the truth. They also need to be reassured that you will be okay, they will be okay, and everything will be okay.

  Most grief experts suggest that it is appropriate for children to attend memorial services. However, viewing a body in a casket may not be appropriate for younger children. They can be given the choice to attend a funeral, burial, or wake; however, they should not be forced to go. Discuss this with your children to understand and address their fears.

- Seek out group resources, such as camps for children who are suffering loss. It is important for your children to see that they aren't the only ones who have lost a loved one. They also need the support of trained adults. Your children may resist, but try to motivate them to attend such groups when they are young. It's harder when they are older and more time has passed.

- Seek out adults, such as teachers, coaches, and church friends, who also lost a parent early in life. Connecting with them can provide strong support for your children.

  However, be sure that these adults are safe people. Educate your children about inappropriate behavior and reassure them that they can talk with you if they feel uncomfortable around a particular adult.

- If you seek counseling for your children under the age of 12, look for someone who specializes in play therapy. Talk therapy is usually not effective in younger children who "talk" through play, not words.

  Your teenagers may be very resistant to therapy and even refuse to talk. Your job as a parent is to get them there; it's the therapist's job to connect with them. Seek a therapist who is experienced with helping teens through grief. Animal-assisted therapy can also be very effective in reaching both children and teens.

- Provide many opportunities for your young children to express their feelings through play. Research shows that a child's active focus is enhanced by playing with an adult. So, play with them using clay, art, pictures, drawing, doll houses, action figures, medical toys, or finger puppets.

  Kids will process their emotions through dramatic play. Don't worry if they start acting out their parent's death. For example, it may seem morbid if the child's doll kills the doctor and saves the daddy. This type of dramatic play is normal. Don't shut it down. Just be curious and interested. "What is happening here? Tell me what happens next. Is there a happy ending?"

  Gently mirror your child's emotions. If he or she is sad, hug them and provide empathy. If they are angry, agree with them. "It IS awful that Mommy died! The cancer WAS a bad, bad thing."

- For your older children, provide art supplies, journals, or music, sports, and dance classes. They need your encouragement to participate in new mediums and opportunities through which to express their emotions.

- Be aware of warning signs in your children's behavior, such as withdrawing from normal life, pushing away friends, or otherwise starting to act differently. This indicates that they need help. It's time to seek a professional, such as a doctor and/or a therapist.

3.  Over time, children of all ages may regress develop-
    mentally. A toddler may go backwards in toilet training. A
    teen may behave in less-mature ways. This is normal, for
    a time. If your child continues to regress or seems "stuck"
    in their development, talk with a doctor or therapist.

4.  Pre-teens, teens and young adults may be at risk for
    acting out their feelings. They might make poor choices,
    engage in risky behavior, or use substances like alcohol
    or drugs to numb their pain. They may want to spend
    money they don't have. Or they may turn to relationships
    of the opposite sex to make up for the loss of a parent.
    Be sure to have good conversations around all of these
    subjects. There are books and programs to help with
    these difficult discussions.

5.  Kids will take their cues about how to grieve from adults
    in their immediate social circle, especially the surviving
    parent. This may be one of the hardest areas for us, as
    parents, to deal with. In the midst of our shock and grief,
    we must still take care of our children and set a good
    example for them. Our children are watching how we
    cope, how we grieve, and how we deal with this tragedy.
    Since they learn more from what we do than what we say,
    parents who model authentic emotional expression, open
    communication, courage, and resilience, will increase the
    odds that their children will also cope and heal well.

6.  Familiar family patterns will emerge in times of crises.
    These behaviors and communication styles will impact
    how we and our children cope with grief.

    Here are some common parenting dynamics:

    - In many families, one parent is the disciplinarian
      and the other the more relaxed, "fun" parent. Losing
      our partner also means losing the role they played
      in parenting. If the relaxed parent remains, he or
      she may need to learn how to create structure. If the
      disciplinarian remains, he or she may need to learn
      more flexibility. Positive parenting programs can
      help the remaining parent to balance these necessary
      elements of grace and truth.

In creating structure, it is important to find a new routine or rhythm as quickly as you can. Children of all ages need structure, routine, expectations, and limits in order to feel safe, loved, and like someone is "in charge." In our grief, there will be times when we cannot maintain our typical schedule or routine. Disciplining children, at such a time, seems like rolling boulders uphill. But the longer chaos is allowed to go unchecked, the more difficult it will be to rein it back in. The Bible says, "Discipline your son, and he will give you peace; he will bring delight to your soul" (Proverbs 29:17). As a suddenly single parent you may need help with this task.

---

*While we cannot control outcomes, implementing the above principles will help us grow through this tragic experience. Then our children can become more resilient, stronger, and find greater meaning, purpose, and hope.*

---

When you are overwhelmed with parenting, it is a signal to take some time for yourself. This is the most responsible thing you can do to benefit your children. Consider enlisting the help of other parents in your support system. Can they babysit your young children while you have an adult conversation with another friend? Can they take your teenager shopping or to the movies? Can you get away for an afternoon, or better yet, overnight to process your own grief? After attending to your own needs, you will find it easier to address the needs of your children.

- Perfection is not the goal of parenting. We can feel guilty about our flaws. But being a "good enough" parent is good enough! Though we may see what appear to be ideal families all around us, it is only an illusion.

While we cannot control outcomes, implementing the above principles will help us grow through this tragic experience. Then our children can become more resilient, stronger, and find greater meaning, purpose, and hope.

Another common parenting pattern after loss is to become permissive and indulgent in an attempt to relieve our children's pain. Resist this urge to replace their grief with activities or material things. These are poor substitutes for the comfort our children need. They want us, not our stuff!

7. One of the most valuable parenting aids is a family meeting. Communication is the glue that binds a family together during a crisis. Holding weekly family meetings provides an opportunity to pray together, to have fun together, to stay current on upcoming commitments and activities, and to celebrate each other's successes. Meetings also provide a safe, respectful environment in which to problem-solve common family challenges such as the distribution of chores and the management of time and transportation. Keeping a family calendar will help reduce misunderstandings and miscommunications that often lead to conflicts.

Widowed parenting presents many challenges. But as we parents become more resilient, so do our children. My favorite definition of resilience is *the ability to bounce forward.* Adversity can propel us into opportunities to become stronger as individuals and as a family. It's more than just surviving or getting through something; it's about thriving and ultimately becoming even better than before.

A common phrase in widowed groups is, "Welcome to the club that nobody wants to join." But we are here. And together, we can learn, grow, and cheer each other along in this difficult, yet ultimately rewarding parenting experience. Depending on where you are in your grief process and current circumstances, this may be hard for you to believe. Hold on! Keep the faith! Know that you and your kids are going to make it! And someday, perhaps, you'll find meaning and purpose by supporting another who has joined the club that nobody wants to join. Then you, too, will be able to say:

Praise be to the God and Father of our Lord Jesus Christ,

the Father of compassion and the God of all comfort, who comforts us in all our troubles, so that we can comfort those in any trouble with the comfort we ourselves have received from God (2 Corinthians 1:3-4).

# Questions for Discussion:

1. What are some examples of good self-care and modeling that you would like to practice and pass on to your children?

_____

_____

_____

_____

_____

_____

_____

_____

2. Based on what you have read here, what are two things you can do to support your children's healing process?

_____

_____

_____

_____

_____

_____

_____

_____

3. What is your biggest fear about parenting your children now? What might you do to calm that fear?

_____

_____

_____

_____

_____

_____

_____

_____

_____

_____

# Chapter 12
*My New Identity*
*by Rev. Gary Vossler, M.Div.*

The death of a loved one can illicit emotions we didn't know existed within us. That certainly happened to me after Sharon, my wife of 41 years, died. Previously, it would have taken a very sad movie or event to bring a tear to my eye. Even then, my tears would have been short-lived and almost undetectable. I made sure of that. I just didn't feel like crying, and I certainly wasn't going to pretend. But then, my wife battled breast cancer off and on for 22 years. With all our children present, she finally passed away right before our eyes. The death of the love of my life overrode my stoic German heritage and background. I never knew what uncontrollable sobbing was until the time of her death. The Scripture says that there is a season for everything, including weeping. And this was my season.

The death of a spouse can feel like an attack on every aspect of our being because the significance of the marriage relationship encompasses what it means to become one-flesh with another human. This experience of loss can be overwhelming, traumatic, and will change us forever. Our personal history, identity and even the fabric of who we are begins to change. This drastic metamorphosis will continue throughout the ensuing months and years.

A month or so after Sharon's death, I drove alone from where I live in Washington state to South Dakota to visit my ailing mother and other family members along my route. I drove 5,500 miles in three and a half weeks through Washington, Idaho, Montana, and the Dakotas. The scenery through these vast expanses was breathtaking, and the April weather was very cooperative! On my way home, I looped down through the Southwest states.

It was on this trip that I felt emotions I didn't know existed. I experienced profound sadness and grief along with guilt and pain to the degree that I had only heard and read about. For hours on end, traveling those desolate highways of eastern Washington, Idaho, Montana, and North Dakota, I sobbed my heart out. I know I probably shouldn't have been driving, because there were untold miles when I didn't even see the road for my tears. I am thankful there was very little traffic during my trip.

It has been 11 years since that road trip, and I have learned and experienced so much since then. After the loss of a spouse, we never completely forget the agony we suffered. We will still feel pain from time to time, but it will be much less frequent and intense. After a while, it won't hurt so much, but the memories will remain, nonetheless.

Healing will take time. While we can facilitate the healing process, we can also do things that slow it down, stop it for a while, or avoid it altogether. If we bury our feelings in drugs, alcohol, or workaholism, we will stop our progress. Even a new love relationship very soon after the death of our loved one can slow our healing.

In working through our own personal journey, it is so good to relive and retell the events and memories we shared with our lost love. Telling our story can help take the sting out of the grief. Some even write letters to their deceased spouse as an aid in saying goodbye.

Many of us feel confusion along with the crying. Others feel anger and clumsiness. I had those feelings because my mind was preoccupied. That made everything slow and awkward. It was as if my computer was trying to run one program while I was looking at another.

I was fortunate to be the recipient of six months of free grief counselling through a cancer care center. My therapist was an older gentleman, very versed in helping the bereaved. Because of his Latvian descent, his unique way of sharing very helpful truths really resonated with me. He said that there are two basic essentials in the grieving process:

1. The first is finding the meaning of life. Your spouse is gone, but you are still here for a reason. God has a purpose for you. He will help you find it.

2. The second is continuing to live while you grieve. You are like a child on the beach who is building a whole new sandcastle. You are being called upon to slowly construct a new life without your loved one.

During this construction season, it is good to cry. Crying is normal, healthy sadness that is expressed through tears. Tears do not mean one is weak! We are humans, not angels. We are not even small cherubim. We will make mistakes along our grief journey. It is helpful to embrace our humanness during this venture. Remember to be good to yourself. This is a wonderful axiom to live by while experiencing grief.

It is very important to pay attention to our minds and hearts and do a lot of talking. My grief counselor said that we learn to live with grief. We must go through the process. He said that if we do anything to block or slow it down, it will only take longer and hurt more. Grief is what it is. The best thing to do is to cooperate with it instead of fighting it. In the end, it will have its way with us.

The truth is that each person must come up with their own architecture as they structure a new life without their loved one. Along the way, we may encounter obstacles in building. We might overfocus on the death process or deny the finality of our spouse's absence. If this is your situation, bereavement counseling can help you process the traumatic events of your spouse's passing. Then you may be more able to accept the reality of their death in such a way that you no longer avoid thinking about it.

> *It is okay to have a strong need for companionship and ask God to fulfill that need. It is also okay to want to live as a single person. Let us give one another grace for whichever way God might lead.*

Now, let's address a topic on the minds of many of the widowed—finding love again. Can we find love after loss? Some are very interested, and others have no inclination whatsoever to marry again. Each one of us is unique in this respect. Since losing my spouse, I have encountered many others who have also been widowed. I would venture to say that about half of them want to find a new love and half will go to their graves remembering the love they had before. This is a totally personal choice and either one is to be celebrated.

In terms of a new relationship, sage advice says to give

oneself plenty of time and space. My wise counselor said that some people grieve more after two or three months than at the beginning. I certainly grieved more the second month than the first because I was on that road trip. Others say it is good to give oneself at least a year before entering a marriage-type relationship.

Getting into a romantic relationship too soon can be treading on very thin ice. It is not fair to the new person when the grieving person is still stuck in the past. Many wonder when they are ready. It really is impossible to put a time frame on preparedness for beginning a new relationship. Everyone is unique, and we all process our grief at our own pace.

There are four areas of compatibility to consider when looking for a significant relationship. These are spiritual, intellectual, physical, and emotional. I learned how to nurture and develop myself in these areas. In his book, "The New Rules for Love, Sex, and Dating," Andy Stanley challenged us to become the kind of person that the person we are looking for is looking for[10]. I discovered the immense importance of becoming whole again. I celebrated the new Gary who eventually emerged out of the rubble and brokenness of grief and pain.

It is okay to have a strong need for companionship and ask God to fulfill that need. It is also okay to want to live as a single person. Whether we decide to remain single or marry again, we can choose to move forward through our grief. We are not "moving on" and leaving our deceased loved one behind. We are "moving forward" by staying single or by asking God for someone new to love. Let us give one another grace for whichever way God might lead us.

It is also important to consider your children who may instinctively want to protect you. They don't want their surviving parent to get hurt. If you choose to enter into a new relationship soon after the death of your loved one, your partner will need to bear your children's feelings in mind and extend extra grace to them.

I have had many discussions with my Savior about remarriage.

---

10      "The New Rules for Love, Sex, and Dating," Andy Stanley, Zondervan, Grand Rapids, MI, 2015.

I have read extensively and searched the Scriptures. As each person studies the Word of God for themselves, they will also sense God's direction for their own life. He is so crazy about us. He loves us so very much that He even counts every hair on our heads. If He is that intimately concerned about us and cares for us to that great extent, He will not abandon us when it comes to loving again, if that is what we desire. He is very much involved in every part of our lives.

I believe marriage to be a Kingdom enterprise ordained by the very heart of God, just as it was in the garden for Adam and Eve. If God calls two people together, He does so because they are more effective in the Kingdom together than they are separately. He ordains our lives in this very important area for His Glory. May God grant us grace as we live to love and serve Him more.

# Questions for Discussion:

1.  What has been your saddest moment in your grief journey?

   _____

   _____

   _____

   _____

   _____

   _____

   _____

   _____

   _____

   _____

2.  How do you feel about finding love again?

   _____

   _____

   _____

   _____

   _____

   _____

   _____

   _____

   _____

   _____

3. What are you doing in the areas of self-nurturing?

_____

_____

_____

_____

_____

_____

_____

_____

_____

_____

# A Final Word

This book is intended to be your guide for first-hand first aid for the first year following the loss of your spouse. Every-one's grief and circumstances are different, but we hope that you have found comfort through our sharing what we've learned through experience.

Grief is only temporary. It is a stage in your life. Grief has a beginning, a middle, and an end. You will come THROUGH the Valley of the Shadow of Death to the other side. We are privileged to walk with you and Jesus through your grief valley into a beautiful, spacious place.

And the God of all grace, who called you to His eternal glory in Christ, after you have suffered a little while, will Himself restore you and make you strong, firm and steadfast (I Peter 5:10).

You will become "oaks of righteousness, a planting of the Lord for the display of His splendor" (Isaiah 61:3b).

You are still here for a reason. God has a plan for your life. After you have surfaced from your grief, you will discover that you have emerged as a new person with an individual identity and purpose. With God's help, you are going to make it!

---

*"I remain confident of this: I will see the goodness of the Lord in the land of the living. Wait for the Lord; be strong and take heart and wait for the Lord"*
*(Psalm 27:13-14).*

# ABOUT THE AUTHORS

**Bruce McLeod**

Bruce has facilitated men's GriefShare groups, and with Chris Taylor, co-authored, ***Take Heart! A Widowed Man's Guide to Growing Stronger.*** Bruce lost his wife Cheri to cancer. His work with The Widows Project constitutes a return as a family missionary, something he and Cheri were called to and worked at consistently until a few weeks before Cheri passed. They facilitated small groups for better relationships, held seminars and inner healing prayer sessions, based on Christian principles.

**Rev. Gary Vossler. M.Div**

Sharon and I met at Moody Bible Institute. We were married for 41 years and served the Lord together in full-time ministry, before she passed away 11 years ago. We had four children and, eventually, 10 grandchildren. I am an ordained minister with an MA of Divinity and postgraduate studies in Pastoral Counseling. I also practice financial advising.

**Joy Ost**

Joy Ost started a career over thirty years ago as a Spanish and English translator and interpreter. Born in the United States, Joy has resided in Mexico most of her life, allowing her a bicultural mindset. She created Word Factor S.C., a company that provides translation, interpreting, and language proficiency learning services to a diverse portfolio of clients. Before that, Joy worked at Aeromexico, participating in the implementation of Club Premier and the SkyTeam alliance.

**Linda Smith, BS**

Linda Smith was married to Kirby for 37 years, and they have two children and six grandchildren. She comes from a background in education, both Christian and secular. She has taught at every age level and has led several widows' support groups since becoming a widow.

**Lisa C. Greene, M.A., CFLE**
When Lisa's husband Carl passed away unexpectedly, she was plunged into the chaos of coping with her own grief and parenting two teenagers alone. Lisa drew upon her professional expertise as a Certified Family Life Educator. Professionally, Lisa is an adjunct professor at Concordia University, a public speaker, author of four books on parenting and has a master's degree in Family Life Education. Her message is: "You can do it!"

**Mary Beth Woll, MA, LMHC**
Mary Beth Woll was married to Bob for almost 39 years before the Lord took him home. Bob and Mary Beth were co-music ministers for 20 years. Together they have four children and eight grandchildren. Mary Beth has a master's degree in counseling/psychology and works as a therapist with Meier Clinics. She also co-authored a book with Paul Meier, M.D., ***Growing Stronger: 12 Guidelines to Turn Your Darkest Hour into Your Greatest Victory.***

**Nancy Honeytree Miller**
Nancy Honeytree Miller has recorded 16 albums and ministers across the US and internationally. She sang her "Call of the Harvest" CD in English, Spanish, and Urdu (of Pakistan). Nancy and her husband J.R. lost their newborn son. Then 23 years later, J.R. went to be with the Lord. Nancy's son, Will, and his family live near her. She currently participates in an online Spanish grief recovery ministry. When at home she leads worship in Fort Wayne, Indiana.

**Chaplain Roberta Reyna, MA**
Roberta married Pedro Reyna and lived in Mexico 29 years working together in church ministry before he died of cancer. She has two master's degrees in education and has taught classes from preschool to university. She has organized and participated in short-term mission trips worldwide, mostly in Mexico. She has two daughters and four grandchildren. Presently, she is collaborating with a group that brings comfort to grieving individuals, and also works as a corporate chaplain.

**Ruth Martinez (Ost)**
**Monterrey Mexico**
Ruth was married to Victor 48 years. She is mother to five children, grandmother, great grandmother, teacher, pastor, counselor, author, advisor, and conference speaker. After becoming a widow, her focus has been to comfort those in grief.

**Rolland Wright,**
**Founder of The Widows Project**
What an honor to be tasked with founding an organization for the widowed community. In seven years, we have achieved much together, and the future is bright. We have become a community of comfort, walking alongside many in their time of loss. May God continue to extend our reach to the grieving across the nations.